RIFF
THE SHAKE KEANE STORY

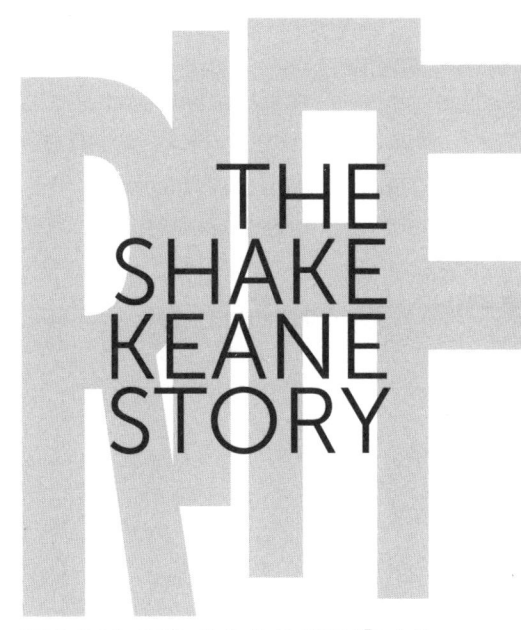

PHILIP NANTON

PAPILLOTE PRESS
London and Trafalgar, Dominica

By the same author

Frontiers of the Caribbean
(Manchester University Press, 2017)

Canouan Suite and Other Pieces
(Papillote Press, 2016)

Island Voices from St Christopher and the Barracudas
(Papillote Press, 2014)

For jazz historian Val Wilmer, a good friend

In memory of Erik Bye (1926-2004)
and Coleridge Goode (1914-2015)

First published by Papillote Press 2021 in Great Britain

© Philip Nanton 2021

The moral right of Philip Nanton to be identified as the author of this work has been asserted by him in accordance with the Copyright, Designer and Patents Act 1988.

All rights reserved. No part of this publication may be reproduced, stored in a retrieval system or transmitted in any form or by any means, electronic, mechanical, including photocopying, recording or otherwise, without the prior permission of the copyright owner.

Printed and bound by CPI Group (UK) Ltd, Croydon CRO 4YY
Book design by Andy Dark
Typeset in Minion

ISBN: 978-1-9997768-9-3

A CIP catalogue record for this book is available from the British Library.

Papillote Press
23 Rozel Road
London SW4 0EY
United Kingdom.
And Trafalgar, Dominica
www.papillotepress.co.uk

CONTENTS

1/ Vee's Snackette - 1

2/ 'Blessed little home-home island'[1] - 7

3/ London is the place for me - 27

4/ Moving on - 53

5/ 'There's no up without a down' - 71

6/ The 'laden garden' of poetry - 81

7/ Crossroads of jazz and poetry - 95

8/ The view from Tiffany's Lounge - 111

Appendices - 128
Discography - 140
Bibliography - 144
Shake Keane Publications - 146
Acknowledgements - 147
Index - 154

Cover photo: Shake Keane playing trumpet and flugelhorn, National Jazz Festival, Richmond, Surrey, 1963. (*Val Wilmer*)

1 Shake Keane, *The Angel Horn: Shake Keane Collected Poems* (St Maarten: House of Nehesi, 2005), 178. Henceforth *Collected Poems*.

Joe Harriott (left) and Shake Keane, National Jazz Festival, Richmond, Surrey, 1963. (*Val Wilmer*)

1/VEE'S SNACKETTE

Shake Keane was back home in St Vincent working as a teacher when I first met him in 1979. In his lunch hour, we would occasionally retreat to the quiet of Vee's Snackette, a tiny bar on the corner of busy Bay and James Street in the island's capital, Kingstown. The bar, surrounded by shops and government offices, was close to the school where Shake was then teaching. (The entire corner block is now a bright but ugly KFC franchise.) Vee's had only two windows, one looking out onto each congested street. Smaller than a one-car garage, the bar was a simple room with a garish melamine-coated counter and three high wooden stools. We were the only customers. Miss Vee, a sturdy, no-nonsense lady, would put out a petit-quart bottle of rum and a small bowl of ice for me. Shake's lunch comprised three bottles of Guinness. She would then leave us alone as she scurried around in a back room.

We exchanged returnee gossip about life in England of the 1960s and the effect of coming back to St Vincent. By this time Shake was sceptical about his return. He had abandoned his flourishing jazz career in Europe and lost out to political manoeuvring in St Vincent over the post he had most wanted and had returned to implement —

Director of Culture for St Vincent and the Grenadines. Sacked from this job after two years and with no other source of income, he felt compelled to accept the first vacant post and became Principal of Bishop's College, a grand name for a small secondary school in Georgetown, the island's second town in the northern Windward district. It seems that even in the relative tranquillity of teaching disaster lurked. At one of our meetings he described almost losing his life when one evening, during his time as Principal, he went to turn on an electric lamp and was hurled across his office. Faulty wiring.

Shake was by then in his early fifties; tall and broad, around six foot four and somewhat shaggy in appearance. His size was emphasised by his characteristic loose-fitting clothing above brown latticed leather sandals. By this time he had a luxuriant grey beard and a thinning head of hair. He moved slowly when the pain of gout struck. A large pair of spectacles rested on his nose below heavy grey eyebrows. Between his long delicate fingers he invariably held a roll-up cigarette. He spoke in a deep baritone voice. This apparently fierce demeanour was softened in conversation by an unassuming smile that came quick and easily.

Vee's Snackette looked directly onto the street. Passersby would see him there and hail the famous musician and returned fellow Vincentian. A celebrated figure in the island, he was used to this public show of interest and would often be stopped in the street. A brief chat was a public sign of connection to a man of international stardom. One lunchtime, a young stevedore, hot and sweaty from the nearby docks, entered the bar:

'Mista Car-heen! Mista Car-heen! 'Cuse me sar. Ah have one sar. Don't mind the clothes all ragga, sar. I just off the jetty. You could hear me sar? Dis one goin be good sar. It go so…

I was liming on the block
wid de boys from de rum shop
is then I bounce up big Mary
them days she frennin Big Nancy'

'OK, OK, pal, enough.'

'It have plenty more verses sar. You like how it going? You could help me fix it up sweet, sweet? Put a lil chorus. Get recording contract and ting…. Or even… a lil drink, den sar? Me troat dry.'

Shake bought him the drink.

Supplicants came in other forms. At one of our meetings I myself showed up with a poem that I'd written. Without hesitation he took out a pen and began deleting words and rearranging its lines, circling sections with arrows going first in one direction then another to different parts of the page, instinctively aiming at bringing the page alive. I like to think I learned something about poetry firsthand from Shake.

At this stage of his life he had been back in St Vincent for six years, after more than 21 years away, first in London then in Germany. Other locations, especially New York and Norway, were to follow. These movements suggest an itinerant — a wanderer who was both framed and influenced by the twentieth century, his lifespan stretching from 1927 to 1997. Indeed, he absorbed and was absorbed by many of the currents flowing through the century. In his chosen fields, especially jazz and poetry, he not only understood them but knew how to excel in them.

Three twentieth-century currents were important in shaping his individual talents and personality. The first of these was the rise of nationalism in the Caribbean. Shake grew up and lived through a time when regional and island national sentiments were at their strongest — expressed in demands for self-government, the rise and fall of regional federation and, finally, the achievement of island-based political independence. This nationalist current was also flowing around the world, touching the colonies from the Caribbean to Africa and Asia. It brought with it political change and a sense of the importance of nation-making which no thinker of the twentieth-century Caribbean could ignore. But when Shake departed St Vincent for England in 1952, the island was still a colonial outpost; only one year earlier it had experienced its first general election under adult suffrage. When he returned in 1973, it was a few years after the island had attained Associated Statehood with Britain (1969). This was, in effect, when locally elected politicians gained control of the island's resources and budget, taking over from the British. Six years after his return, St Vincent gained full political independence. If, as a young man, Shake had left a colony, he returned to a place in which local people vied for influence and power and local party politics was ruthless. He returned, therefore, to a different island from the one he had left.

The second great current in which Shake was caught up was the experience of migration. The question facing all migrants of 'where is home?' becomes especially urgent for a doubly displaced person. As someone who spent the first 25 years of his life in St Vincent, Shake was born into one diaspora. He then lived in England and in Europe for 21 years as a member of another; he returned to his birthplace for eight years before migrating yet again to live the last 16 years of his life in New York. His return to St Vincent captures a common dilemma experienced by many migrants — the desire to offer service 'back home' versus self-fulfilment in the adopted country. When such an itinerant is a sensitive professional musician for whom travel to different venues and countries is almost a daily constant, the question of home and homecoming has even more resonance. Not surprisingly, home and the challenges of migration are important themes in his poetry. His early writing begins by celebrating place before becoming, later, a poetry of *dis*placement, playing with multiple positions in relation to the conundrum of home. In tracing this second contextual current we shall see how Shake's physical movements and creative responses constitute a form of mapping.

The third current that shaped his identity was masculinity. By masculinity I do not mean a fixed and limited way of behaving — as though there were only one way to 'be a man' — but a range of performances, as man, musician, teacher and poet, through which he searched for a role and a sense of self. His masculinity was tested by his failure to realise his full potential in the jazz world of the 1960s, modest recognition for his poetry, and finally a conventional and serial dependence on the women closest to him. Sometimes the performances coalesced and sometimes they contradicted one another. These currents — nationalism, migration and masculinity — are, of course, intimately connected. Taken together, they have a peculiar power in animating Shake Keane's life.

At the same time, his mature performances, especially as musician and poet, are shaped by innovative presentations that are difficult to pin down. In this way he disrupts the clear lines of demarcation between styles and genres that critics often require. Located at the crossroads between jazz and poetry, Shake's most significant achievement was ultimately a blurring of the boundaries between these two art forms.

St Vincent Grammar School Cadet Band, Halifax Street (Back Street), Kingstown, 1950s. (*Courtesy Clifford Edwards*)

2 / 'BLESSED LITTLE HOME-HOME ISLAND'

We were children
when corked hats and plumed feathers
were among the heights of fashion
when you walked to church to hear a preacher's sermon
and teaching was a serious profession
clinking the keys to our future.[1]

'Shake' Keane was born Ellsworth McGranahan Keane on 30 May 1927 in Kingstown. He was the third son and fifth of seven children of Charles E Keane (1869-1941) and Dorcas Maude née Edwards (nd - 1963) widely known as 'Jessie'. The total number of children that Charles fathered is uncertain — Shake claimed 'many' half siblings. He said that his father had been married twice before his marriage to Jessie. The registry office lists only six children from the marriage of Charles and Dorcas. His older siblings were Hadassah Magdalin Roxann, Theodore Vanragin, Edna Elaine, McIntyne Wilberforce, then there was Shake, Donny (unlisted) and Darnell Mendelssola. Certainly, Charles and Jessie were attracted to grand names for their offspring.

The family was culturally rich but economically poor. His father was a self-educated man who managed money badly and held a variety of jobs. Two were significant: he worked at different times as an estate overseer and as a corporal in the Royal St Vincent Police.[2] In the countryside, where Charles was based before moving to Kingstown, both jobs held authority and power. According to Shake, these positions of local status also accounted for Charles's substantial but unquantified extended family.

Music as an interest came about by chance while Charles was living and working in the countryside. The three prominent positions in the island's rural villages at this time were the police corporal, the school principal and the estate overseer. With few diversions and no electricity, these three authority figures would get together most evenings. As Shake told it, the Principal, a Mr Drayton, an able musician from Barbados, offered to teach Charles the rudiments of music. Charles had an aptitude and soon could read music, hold a note and play the trumpet. And so music was born as an occupation in the Keane household. It is not known what year Charles moved to Kingstown, but both the marriage of Charles and Dorcas as well as the birth of their first child were officially registered in Kingstown in 1916.

It is possible that in recognition of the family's religious affiliations as Methodists and love of music, Charles and Dorcas gave their third son the middle name of McGranahan after James McGranahan, the nineteenth-century American composer of hymns, whom Charles admired. The first name, Ellsworth, popular in the first decade of the twentieth century, is derived from the Old English name Ellias and evokes nobility. With names such as 'Ellsworth' and 'McGranahan', it is perhaps not surprising that he was more often known in his early years by his nicknames: firstly, 'Muz', possibly short for 'music' given his public performances at an early age, and later 'Shake'. He answered to 'Muz' Keane throughout his early school and teaching days and even when signing letters to friends. But over time, 'Shake' was the name that stuck. There are at least two versions of its origins. According to one story, it is a diminutive of 'Shakespeare', given to him by school friends and musicians in honour of his love of literature. Another story links it to his fondness for a particular Duke Ellington tune of the 1940s in which the trumpet features prominently — 'Chocolate Shake'. Whichever version is true, the nickname alludes to his three great passions: music, English literature and the poetry of the Caribbean.

Early twentieth-century Kingstown was a mixture of poverty and aspiration. Unlike modern Kingstown with its concrete and glass business structures, the town centre then comprised both residences and places of work, often in the same building. In the 1930s only a few public streets had electric lights, and at night homes were lit by candles and oil lamps. The core of the capital was its three main streets. Bay Street and Back Street sandwiched Middle Street, in the lower section of which — called Lower Middle Street — the Keane family lived. Homes and businesses for the most part were small clapboard houses comprising ground and first floor. The family home was located in a lively artisanal area with open gutters running on both sides of the street. There were two blacksmiths nearby, as well as a small printery. From his upstairs bedroom window Shake could see into a nearby bakery, where the sweat poured off the backs of bakers kneading dough for their ovens. In the neighbourhood could be found two brass bands — the Keane family band and Cyril McIntosh's Brass Band — as well as Melody Makers Steel Band, and further up the street Syncopators Steel Band.[3] Black families, like the Keanes, could be classified as artisans aspiring to middle-class status, with homes slightly removed from the town's administrative centre.

Nearer the centre of the town could be found wealthier middle-class families. Their stone-walled houses were primarily residential, characterised by cooling arches that supported overhead balconies. White planters and business people, who often intermarried, represented the island's elite and lived in those houses close to the town centre until the mid-twentieth-century fashion of living outside the capital took hold.

Despite these contrasts, the St Vincent of Shake's birth was a small outpost, often referred to in colonial parlance as a 'minor colony'. In 1927 the island had 49,751 inhabitants.[4] It was run by an administrator from Britain and three elected and nominated local members of the island's Legislative Council. The electoral roll was tiny and based on land ownership, and nominated members were white planters who invariably sided with the colonial authorities. In his annual report for 1927, the Administrator, Robert Walter, expressed his pride that the island's finances were stable. The economy was essentially agricultural and his main concern was that someone should establish a hotel to kick-start a tourist industry. His pitch for tourism in the official yearbook was based on the charm of St Vincent's volcanic mountains and the character of its people. 'The people of St Vincent,' he claimed, 'are extremely warm-hearted, law-abiding, simple and in many ways most attractive and lovable.'[5] In fact, the social reality and political undercurrents were considerably different from this official view of island tranquillity.

In 1935, when Shake was eight, Kingstown erupted in a riot — the immediate cause of which was a protest against the insensitivity of the colonial administration in imposing a local tax on household matches. Afflicted by poverty and lack of work, ordinary people feared that a tax on such a basic commodity would worsen their already difficult plight. In October that year, attempts by the region's

Governor, Selwyn MacGregor Grier, to deny the negative impact of the tax, as he tried to negotiate with a restless crowd gathered in front of the island's Court House, singularly failed. Fearing that the Governor, who was in charge of the Windward Islands, including St Vincent, would depart the island for his residence in Grenada before the issue was settled, voices were raised, business houses wrecked and policemen were beaten and trampled. In turn, the police fired their guns above and into the crowd. Rioting led to days of looting of shops in Kingstown and Georgetown as well as threats to white planters, and the call for a British naval gunboat to help restore order. The reality that underlay the riot was severe long-term poverty and unemployment for the island's poorer urban and rural black working class, who did not have the option of obtaining land to secure a livelihood.

The rioters probably had less to lose than the aspirational and relatively respectable black urban strata in which the Keane family were located. As a one-time police officer, Charles's sympathies are unlikely to have been on the side of the protesters. The family were regular churchgoers and Charles often organised singing evenings in neighbours' homes. These features of the Keane family suggest that Charles's aims for the family were geared more towards self-improvement than political action.

However, not all family members were quiescent. From an early age Shake expressed through his music a commitment to his island's development. He and his brother Don played at the rallies of the Working Men's Co-operative Association (WMCA), to enliven the crowd prior to speeches and hustings for the Legislative Council elections. The WMCA set up co-operative groups and helped informally in labour negotiations. Popular with grass-roots voters, the WMCA won four of the five seats in the 1937 election for membership of the island's Legislative Council. Also, from Shake's early published writing it is clear that he was a committed regionalist who looked forward to federation. This view was modified in later life when he argued the benefits of 'gradual arrangements to come together.'[6]

Charles taught each of his children to read music, to sing and play a musical instrument.[7] With his police-force background, he was a strict disciplinarian, and Shake described his father's teaching methods as 'a very gruelling process'. He offered his own childhood experience as an example: 'I had every night to recite various things from the theory of music and the theory of the trumpet. I knew a lot about the trumpet, how to hold it and how to carry it in the street, how to march with it. What notes were produced with what valves — long before I was allowed to put the trumpet to my lips.'[8] Shake remembered a piano being in the home for a while which his older siblings were taught to play. He claimed that it was sold on because of his father's improvident ways. So the younger ones, Shake included, had little choice of instrument; it was the trumpet. The children were subjected to an almost militaristic musical training, with scales to be practised, the trumpet's embouchure to be mastered for pitch and ornamentation, and musical notation to be read, absorbed and examined.

Under his father's tutelage Shake joined the family brass band — playing in public for the first time at the age of six. Many years later, he recounted the experience of playing in the island's Boy Scouts' band — perhaps at an Empire Day parade held on 24 May each year. This official annual holiday was first introduced in the colonies in 1905 to promote loyalty among the dominions of the British Empire and was directed in particular at schoolchildren. As a sign of colonial loyalty, a procession of Church Lads' brigades as well as other Church groups would march past the Administrator, the monarch's representative, at an appointed time at the town's Victoria Park, then an open green space partly surrounded by palm trees. The parade was followed by the Administrator's speech to the assembled groups. Shake described how, when the band marched through Kingstown, handicapped by his short stride he had to run to catch up with the rest of the band members, much to the amusement of bystanders.[9]

At the age of 11, he joined Ted Lawrence and His Silvertone Orchestra, essentially a brass band that played at public dances around the island. Louis Armstrong's 78rpm records were an early influence on the band's repertoire, along with imported score sheets with compositions by American big bands led by Tommy Dorsey, Glen Miller and Benny Goodman. While most of the band dressed in formal suits, the trumpeter, too young for evening dress, wore shorts.[10] The fact that Shake was not afraid to relate such stories showed a willingness not to take himself too seriously.

Shake attended the Methodist Church's primary school in Kingstown, known in St Vincent as the Wesley Hall School. The school was close to his home in Lower Middle Street and his first teacher was Cadman Fraser, himself a musician and trumpeter, who also led the school's Empire Day marches. Formal education was a priority in the Keane household; reading and discussions on many subjects were valued activities, and from the beginning Shake learned to love literature.[11]

With the emphasis at home on a combination of music, reading and strict discipline, Shake received educational advantages denied many pupils at his school. However, getting a place at secondary school for a family on a low budget was not easy. Secondary education had to be paid for and so, with limited means, a scholarship was essential. Starting in 1911, a number of scholarships were offered annually: three secondary scholarships were provided by the colonial government, and single scholarships were offered by the Kingstown Board, the Anglican and Methodist Churches and the Reeves Memorial Scholarship Fund. The competition was stiff for the one scholarship available from the Methodist School. Shake took the exam, and, in 1941, was successful at his third attempt. The year he won was also the one when, in the space of two weeks, his voice transitioned from alto to bass.

The Boys' Grammar School (BGS), the leading secondary school for boys, was located on the outskirts of Kingstown. Founded in 1908, it opened with 13 pupils; by Shake's time there were over 150. The BGS aimed to educate the upper echelons of the island's middle class and to prepare pupils to enter a range of professions. The school's educational model was that of an elite English grammar school, with prefects, strict discipline and corporal punishment. Latin and French were compulsory subjects and the curriculum also included English, Elementary Mathematics, Geography, General Science, Agriculture and Bible Studies. Junior pupils wore khaki shorts and shirts. After a sixth form was established in 1945, these older boys soon had a more distinctive uniform: thick green blazers and heavy grey flannel trousers more suited to a cold climate.

Shake enjoyed learning languages and discovered that he had a particular affinity for French. He found practical ways of extending his French conversation and vocabulary by interacting with French-speaking visitors to St Vincent, such as sailors from Martinique and Guadeloupe. He obtained his School Certificate in 1944. The following year Shake and 11 others entered the newly established sixth form. By 1946 only two students remained, one of whom was Shake. He pursued his studies in French at this higher level and extended his knowledge by listening to a French radio station broadcasting from Quebec. This experience proved invaluable when he returned to the school in 1947 to teach the subject to lower forms.[12]

When Shake was 14, he and his siblings suffered the early death of their father on 11 November 1941. The loss of the main breadwinner was both a tragedy and an economic crisis. To make ends meet, his mother, Jessie, went out to work. But the family's investment in music and education had practical benefits: the family brass band provided some income and Shake was earning by playing in a variety of bands on Friday and Saturday nights, including the Ted Lawrence Band and the Mellow Tones, the latter managed by Frank Rojas, a businessman and radio enthusiast. From 1946 to 1951, Shake was also playing in the St Vincent Philharmonic Orchestra. Patterned on metropolitan orchestras, it played classical music at informal open-air concerts on Sunday afternoons in Georgetown and Barrouallie, a coastal town in the west of the island. The orchestra also played at official colonial occasions, such as the Empire Day parades and at the funerals of prominent Vincentians. Its members included Harold and Tom McIntosh, Frank and Henry Williams, Willy Boyea, Darrow Daisley, Leo Smith, Vin Cato and Winston Samuels. The careful recording of their names testifies to the prestige attached to this level of performance.[13]

Despite its size and limited access to the outside world throughout the late nineteenth and early twentieth centuries, St Vincent produced musicians who could play in a variety of styles. As early as 1893, for example, Kingstown had an established orchestra of brass, woodwind and strings, led by its conductor Rev EJ Holt. This orchestral tradition was maintained until the mid-twentieth century. Socially, the diverse experience of playing at night clubs, in the island's annual street carnival, the pre-Lenten Mardi Gras, and in more formal music-making, brought Shake into contact with both the average working man and woman and the good and great of the island. At the same time, his mastery of formal music as well as popular band music was an invaluable grounding for his later jazz and big-band career in Europe. While music-making had a degree of prestige attached to it — and, as a result, band members were invariably male — there was no potential for making music a full-time career in St Vincent. Anyway, Shake had other ideas: he wanted to master the discipline of English literature.

The seeds of this interest started at home. In the evenings, entertainment for the most part had to be produced among the family. It was commonplace for families to entertain themselves by storytelling, recounting folktales and the legendary Anancy stories. Shake discovered that from a young age he had a facility for rhyme and for telling stories in Vincentian dialect. He soon started to submit poems to the local newspaper, *The Vincentian*, and to *Yuletide*, a literary magazine that for a few years appeared around Christmas time.

One of Shake's boyhood friends from the BGS was Sir Cecil Cyrus, who recognised Shake's linguistic ability from an early age. Cecil was the son of the owner of a well-known men's outfitters called The Cyrus Emporium in Kingstown. Cecil and Shake were first thrown together in Form 2A of the BGS. 'When we were school boys at Grammar School,' said Cyrus, who studied medicine at Queen's University, Belfast, and went on to become a celebrated doctor in St Vincent:[14] 'We would sit on the steps of my father's workplace and plan our futures.' Cyrus's goal was to become a surgeon; one that he achieved with great success. Shake's goal was to go to university to study English literature. This was no surprise to Cyrus, who had long been aware of Shake's facility with words — 'a man who could convince you of anything'[15] — and he was certain that Shake was bound for a literary career.

Another boyhood friend from the BGS who became significant in

Teachers of St Vincent Boys' Grammar School, 1950, Shake Keane is fourth from right. (*Henry Neblett/courtesy Tony Hadley*)

Shake's life was Sir James 'Son' Mitchell, later Prime Minister of St Vincent and the Grenadines. Son, as he is widely known, was born in Bequia, the second largest of the island chain that comprises St Vincent and the Grenadines. The Mitchell family, prominent people in Bequia, were seafarers and landowners and, in Caribbean terms, relatively well off. Son won a scholarship to study abroad, first in Canada and then in Britain where he trained as an agronomist. Two years younger than Shake, he was, like Cecil, a bright and committed student of science. Son's friendship with Shake was first established at the BGS and then developed in London. Their friendship remained a permanent feature and would have a profound effect on Shake's mature life (see Chapter 5).

On completing his Higher School Certificate, Shake left school and joined the island's civil service; and in 1947 took up a post as a magistrate's clerk in Kingstown. For many young people of his generation entering the public service was a prized goal: it conveyed status, and offered a regular salary and an escape from poverty. But for Shake, the routine and conformity were stifling and by the following year he had returned to the BGS as a full-time teacher without formal training. This was not an unusual career path and he remained teaching at the BGS until he left for London in 1952. He taught French and music, and organised a school choir and a school band. But school teaching was not the limit of his ambition. In 1950 he embarked on a correspondence course in English literature with the extramural department of London University, which, he hoped, would lead to a BA degree.

When Shake returned to studying he wrote to Cyrus, who had already left the island to pursue his medical degree. With some apparent irony, he told his friend: 'Can you believe it I'm a *stoodent* (sic). By the grace of God and the salvation of a 60 watt, I am making a regular 5 hours per nite (sic). Not bad for a beginner, eh?'[16] Undertaking this type of study in St Vincent in the 1950s as an extramural student was a slow and laborious process. It involved ordering books from overseas and sending off essays in the post for assessment. Though no qualification followed from this experience, it indicated his commitment to higher education.

As a young black man growing up in urban St Vincent, Shake would have been aware of the political currents that swirled around the island. Pressures for universal suffrage, regional unification and anti-colonial sentiments were gathering force. Underlying these was the extreme poverty and the racial antipathy that was never too far from the surface. In times of tension, in a racially stratified society like St Vincent, with a predominantly black mass and white colonial and planter elite population, racial divisions became more pronounced.[17] In addition, the Italian/Abyssinian war (1935-36) was closely followed by locals who hung around the telegraph station in Kingstown to discover the latest news of the events taking place in Ethiopia. This was another black country taking on its white oppressors by force and, as the island's colonial administrator reported to London, there was a clear sense that the white race had gone to war with the black race in Africa. At the local level, emerging political leaders like the pharmacist George McIntosh and, later, Jonathan Charles and Ebenezer Joshua, returned migrants radicalised by trade union experience in the oil fields of Aruba, were agitating for greater equality at the polls and in the society at large.

Along with these undercurrents, Caribbean colonies such as St Vincent were increasingly aware that the seeds of self-government would lead to direct control of island resources and so, in turn, enable fairer distribution of wealth. The Grenadian journalist and regionalist Theophilus (Teddy) Albert Marryshow often toured St Vincent promoting ideas of island self-government and regional federation. In fact, Marryshow had just departed the island a few days before the 1935 riot in Kingstown.

There were also other signs of regionalism. Between 1926 and 1952 sea routes were established throughout the eastern Caribbean. Three Canadian-owned steam ships — *Lady Nelson, Lady Hawkins* and *Lady Drake* — informally called the 'Lady' boats, passed through the islands every two weeks from Halifax in Canada down to (then British Guiana) Guyana, facilitating travel by carrying passengers as well as cargo.

Geographical and political regionalism was paralleled by the development of a regional sense of literature. Many of the creative writers of the 1940s and 1950s in the Caribbean saw themselves as contributing to this development. It was a literature that focused on island specificity as well as a 'West Indian' identity transcending singular island identities. By the early 1950s, evidence of a commitment to regional writing in St Vincent was there in the work of Shake and two other Vincentian poets, Daniel Williams and Owen

Campbell, who all began to publish their poems in *The Vincentian*, then the only regular outlet in the island. Their work also appeared in *Bim*, edited by Frank Collymore in Barbados, and in *Kyk-Over-Al*, edited by A J Seymour in Guyana. This in turn led to broadcasts on the influential weekly BBC radio programme, *Caribbean Voices*, edited by Henry Swanzy in London.

Caribbean Voices became perhaps the most important focus for the development and promotion of the region's literary output. The idea for a Caribbean literary radio programme had originated with the Jamaican poet and feminist, Una Marson, who, from 1943 to 1945, was its first presenter and producer, followed, for the next eight years, by Swanzy. Swanzy's enthusiasm and skills as a producer converted a programme that started out broadcasting published work into one that was, in effect, a creative workshop for new writing; crucially, it also offered payment for struggling, isolated writers and a platform for criticism of their work. It took the form of a weekly oral magazine of poems, short stories, plays and reviews of writing from the region and beamed them back to the region. Later, Shake would work on *Caribbean Voices* during his early years in London (see Chapter 3).

Of the three Vincentian poets, Campbell's writing appeared the most regularly, with 15 poems published in *Bim* from 1950 to 1967. The titles of Campbell's poems — 'The Washerwomen', 'This Land', 'Hurricane', 'Passage', 'Night Spot', 'And By These Hills' — suggest a direct and secular approach to local, and by implication, regional, subject matter, which perhaps heightened their appeal. Campbell taught in secondary school before eventually emigrating to live in Canada.

Williams's poems appeared in six issues of *Bim* where he published nine poems in all. These evinced a sense of protest with strong religious overtones. He studied law in England and, in the 1960s, when he returned to St Vincent, was part of the Kingstown Study Group. The Group had established the literary magazine *Flambeau* (1964-1968) and supported socialist and black nationalist causes. Williams promoted his ideas and poetry through the magazine, which he edited (along with Kenneth John, the local University of the West Indies tutor). He suffered an early death from a car crash in 1971.

While all three poets drew on local subjects in their writing, there was no unanimity of views among them. For example, in contrast to Williams's black nationalism, Shake argued that the society he was responding to in his writing was identifiably creole, meaning inextricably mixed or hybrid, with the suggestion that a new society was being created: 'No matter how many strains of culture have gone into the making of West Indian people, and because of the variety of these strains, a unique society is being evolved here, with a peculiar system of attitudes, a peculiar reaction to facts and sights and circumstances.'[18]

Despite these differences, the three poets shared a close bond and supported one another's work. Williams reviewed Shake's first collection of poems, *L'Oubli: Poems* in *Bim*, in 1952. Shake dedicated his short folk play *Nancitori With Drums* (1972) to Danny Williams. He later dedicated his prize-winning *One A Week With Water* to Owen Campbell. In this collection, both Williams and Campbell are briefly memorialised for their wit. Shake noted that the statement 'Children's Day. Any Day' was 'A favourite saying of Owen Campbell's —Vincentian poet/friend. Eccentric, now, unfortunately, grown up.'[19] Of Daniel Williams, he recollected: '"The boys and girls of today are the men and women of tonight." Said to me for one week in 1947 by the late Danny Williams, poet/lawyer/friend, when I first took up teaching.'[20]

Each of these three poets in their own way wrote poetry distinguished by a sense of local commitment. And so the beginnings of an identifiable school of poetry was being shaped, characterised by a strong sense of place and their position in it. This commitment is captured, for example, by Owen Campbell's poem, 'We'.

We have decided
Not to construct hope on continents
Or leave lost hearts to rove
In the quick air on oceans of dreams
We have decided to build here in the slender dust.[21]

And in a more politically pointed way in Williams's poem, 'Song of the Peasant':

To the peasant we owe our very existence
In these colonial lands of battered agriculture.[22]

Shake made a considered contribution to this regional groundswell in a discussion paper delivered at a local meeting of the Wesley Guild in Kingstown in September 1950. He began by rebutting the assessment made by Henry Swanzy, who had claimed in a 1949 *Caribbean Voices* broadcast: 'I do not think there is as yet any clear sign of a definite West Indian literature.'[23] While Shake accepted that the literary roots of the language were European, the writing, he argued, had a distinct West Indian flavour. He drew on the writing of regional writers and thinkers like Aimé Césaire (Martinique), Harold Telemaque (Trinidad), Derek Walcott (St Lucia) and Arthur Seymour (Guyana) to support his argument that a body of literature had grown up in the previous 20 years that was definitely West Indian, if not so much in language, in spirit and purpose. He suggested that its imagery was unique and that there was an element of mystery in pre-Columbian place names like 'Warrawarra, Yambou and Kaietur'. Ultimately, what underlies Caribbean writing, he suggested, was its exuberant optimism, which was 'part and parcel of every truly West Indian writer'.[24]

Intra-regional literary contact extended beyond what was made accessible through small magazine publications. Shake recollected to me, for example, that in his early writing days he and the young Derek Walcott in St Lucia occasionally exchanged letters discussing each other's poetry. The publication of Shake's first two books of poetry in Barbados and Guiana respectively was part of the fledgling process of intra-regional publishing. In 1950, through Frank Collymore's help, the Advocate Company in Barbados printed *L'Oubli: Poems*, which sold at $1 per copy. In 1952, Master Printery in High Street, Georgetown, British Guiana, printed his second collection, *Ixion*. This publication was part of the 'Miniature Poets' series facilitated by AJ Seymour of *Kyk-Over-Al*. Each 16-page booklet in the series sold at one shilling per copy. The publication and distribution of the series was described in a *Kyk-Over-Al* editorial as follows: 'The poet being published paid for some copies to be printed and the rest were taken up each month by friends, well wishers, teachers etc.'[25] Some 15 publications were put out in this series, representing writers from Guyana, Grenada, Jamaica, Trinidad, Barbados, and Shake from St Vincent.

By the age of 25, although he was making great strides with his music, Shake's preferred interest lay in literary and intellectual pursuits, reinforced by his six-year commitment to secondary school teaching. This is apparent from the letter to his friend Cecil Cyrus about returning to being a student, as well as his growing list of publications. Such literary achievements suggest someone who had outgrown his island. His realism about the limited opportunities for further intellectual development it afforded him was no doubt a factor in his migration. There was only one government university scholarship for the island available every four years and he felt he 'lacked the wherewithal to grasp and make the most of opportunities'. And so, as he stated later: 'I told myself that I was going to London to study.'[26] In the event, Europe held out a very different future from the one he had envisioned.

Notes

1 Philip Nanton, extract from "Travels," unpublished poem, 2004.
2 Shake Keane, interview by David Austin, New York, 1995.
3 Austin, interview.
4 Robert Walter. *The Yearbook of the Bermudas, The Bahamas, British Guyana, British Honduras and the British West Indies*, (Canada Gazette Ltd, 1928), 297.
5 Walter, Yearbook, 1928, 297.
6 Austin, interview.
7 Charles Keane also taught his wife, Jessie, to play the trumpet. Little else is known about her.
8 Canute James, "Shake Keane All Over - Shake Keane talks to Canute James," *Melody Maker*, January 20, 1973.
9 Dick Pixley, "Musicians of the Caribbean: Shake Keane," *Flamingo*, June 1963, 34-35.
10 Val Wilmer, "Ellsworth McGranahan (Shake) Keane (1927-1997) Jazz Musician and Poet," *Oxford Dictionary of National Biography* (Oxford: Oxford University Press, 2004).
11 It was not surprising that, as well as Shake, his siblings also prospered. His older brother, Theodore, became St Vincent's deputy governor-general; McIntyne became a physical education instructor. Two sisters emigrated to New York and took up careers in social work.
12 Austin, interview.
13 The list is from an encomium *Senior Citizen of Culture… Shake Keane* by Errol G King for the Council of St Vincent and the Grenadines, New York City, 27 October 1996. Shake was 'saluted' for 'his contribution to the Vincentian community at home and abroad… in the fields of music, teaching, poetry and culture in general.' Dr Eitel Providence was also 'saluted' at the same occasion.
14 He was awarded a knighthood in the UK's New Year's honours list, 2019.
15 Cecil Cyrus, interview by the author, St Vincent, 2001.
16 Shake Keane, letter to Cecil Cyrus, November 25, 1950.
17 The colonial authorities had been sufficiently panicked by the 1935 unrest to report to London the overheard comment, 'We goin lick all you white people up tonight.'

18 Ellsworth McG. Keane, "Some Religious Attitudes in West Indian Poetry," *Bim* 4, no.16 (1952): 266.
19 Ellsworth McG. Keane, *One A Week With Water: Rhymes and Notes* (Havana: Ediciones Casa de las Américas, 1979), 59. Hereafter *OWWW*.
20 Keane, *OWWW*, 57.
21 Owen Campbell, "We," *Bim* 4, no.14 (1951): 94-95.
22 Daniel Williams, "Song of the Peasant," *Bim* 4, no.14 (1951): 98.
23 Henry Swanzy, "The Last Six Months," *Caribbean Voices*, BBC radio, 1949.
24 Ellsworth McG. Keane, "The Contribution of the West Indian to Literature," *Bim* 4, no.14 (1951): 102.
25 Arthur J. Seymour, "Editorial note," *Kyk-Over-Al*, 2 (1955): 3.
26 Austin, interview.

Album cover, 1965. (*Courtesy Roland Ramanan*)

3/ LONDON IS THE PLACE FOR ME

To reach up. For years kept reaching up
then something taps me on the shoulder
it's been tapping there a long time.
Before, I could ignore it, that tapping.
It catches me anywhere.[1]

Shake travelled from St Vincent to England in 1952 on the steamship *Colombie*. This trip, like many others following on the heels of the *Empire Windrush*, was becoming a regular journey for West Indians hoping to escape unemployment at home and to find better opportunities in Britain. On its four-week voyage to the motherland, it stopped in Trinidad and Barbados to pick up more immigrants.

In Barbados, where the boat stopped long enough for Keane to get off, he met Frank Collymore for the first time. Collymore asked him: 'What work are you going to do?' He claimed that this question had not occurred to him and without thinking he answered, 'Music.'[2] Collymore also provided him with a letter of introduction to Henry Swanzy at the BBC. The connection with the BBC proved to be invaluable, socially as well as financially.

Where he first stayed on arrival in London is not known but he had little money — he claimed he had no more than £11 in his pocket (the average weekly wage was then £9). With only his limited finances and Collymore's letter to Swanzy, he made an early visit to the Employment Exchange. He was also a black man from the Caribbean joining the existing West Indian population of an estimated 17,000,[3] an outsider in a white British environment that increasingly expressed its anti-black racism. However, unlike many immigrants who were mainly working class with a basic education, Shake had additional assets that would stand him in good stead: he was well read and a published poet; he had a thirst for knowledge and the intention to pursue a degree in literature; he had an ability to read music and play the trumpet; a grounding in Latin from his secondary school and a good knowledge of French. All these skills and abilities were beyond many of the native white population.

Swanzy would have known Shake's name as he had broadcast his poetry when he was writing from St Vincent. *Caribbean Voices* had also aired a critical review by John LaPage about the writing of the Vincentian trio — Shake Keane, Daniel Williams and Owen Campbell — that drew attention to their shared sense of local commitment. So, with his arrival in London, Shake's breakthrough was provided by the BBC. He began as a freelance 'outside broadcaster', covering exhibitions, reading scripts on *Caribbean Voices* and preparing contributions for *We See Britain*, a segment within a weekly magazine programme, *Calling the West Indies*, that introduced West Indians to British lifestyles. He stayed with the BBC on a part-time basis from 1952 to 1965. In this way, Shake was not only a writer from St Vincent, but also a presenter and behind-the-scenes contributor in London. And so he joined the milieu of Caribbean writers, Andrew Salkey from Jamaica, Sam Selvon and VS Naipaul from Trinidad, Edgar

Mittelholzer from Guyana, and George Lamming and Edward (later 'Kamau') Brathwaite from Barbados, who were, like him, all working part-time at the BBC. Here, his sense of regional identity would have been reinforced as one of those West Indian migrants of the 1950s discovering common ground in London.

By the time he resigned from the BBC in 1965, because, his first wife, Christiane, claimed, he had got bored with the work, his musical career had taken off and studio recordings and touring were making substantial claims on his time.

Early black and white pictures of Shake in London and continental Europe show a tall, athletic but also studious-looking black man, with dark rimmed spectacles and a shallow beard — though by 1960 it had become large and bushy. Life was busy and varied for the budding musician. His time was taken up with interviewing or reading scripts for the two weekly BBC programmes; family commitments; playing with pop bands; and then, when he joined the Joe Harriott Quintet there were fortnightly rehearsals at Dynely's Rehearsal Rooms, off Marylebone High Street; he also took up photography alongside his occasional poetry writing and two years of undergraduate study at University College, London.

He had applied and, in 1958, obtained a place at the University of Hull. However, by now he was well settled in London with Christiane, a young French woman whom he had married in 1954, and their elder son, Alan, also born that year. So, in 1959, he enrolled instead at University College, London, for a degree in English literature. He completed two years of the course before it lost out to his developing jazz career. When he was asked about this decision by the journalist Dick Pixley, of *Flamingo* magazine, he put it like this: 'An honours degree in English or fill out my musical career as a pioneer in this revolutionary new sound? After two years the University lost.'[4]

But while he was a student he quickly became a major influence on the University's jazz band, helping them to win an inter-university musical contest in 1960. Anthony Harkavy, a fellow competitor (now a retired solicitor) who played clarinet in Cambridge University's band 'The Southside Six' remembers clearly the circumstances. 'Our first band', he writes, 'containing such luminaries as Art Themen, Dave Gelly and Patrick Gowers, was outstanding and was a pretty strong favourite. I reckoned without the London University Band in general and Shake Keane in particular. Nobody in that auditorium — bar the London contingent — was prepared for the impact which his contribution was to make. From the very first note blown out of his flugelhorn the audience was mesmerised. The purity of tone, the dazzling technique and his musicality were of another order. Sensational. It was to be no contest.'[5]

The abandonment of his degree was a backward step in the eyes of his old friend Cecil Cyrus. He recalled visiting Shake in London and being extremely disappointed at what he saw. 'Here was a man, who had come to do a degree. But when I visited his flat he was at that time interested in, of all things, photography. We were poor persons who had to make sacrifices. I told him we have responsibilities to make something of ourselves. In those days there weren't many chances, you had to take them. I could not conceive of anything distracting him from his goal of obtaining a degree, so he could become a West Indian giant.'[6]

Cyrus underestimated his friend for it was as a jazz trumpeter and flugelhorn player that he would achieve greatness, first in England and then in Europe.

A black male jazz trumpeter is never 'just' a musician, and even the instrument he plays has come to be associated with masculinity and perhaps specifically black masculinity. Also, because of its volume and range, the trumpet is often associated with leadership. In the United States especially, the jazz trumpet has long been identified with black masculinity — stereotypically bringing to mind the dramatic sound of Louis Armstrong, the 'cool' of Miles Davis or the rhythmic virtuosity of the 'clown prince' of the instrument, Dizzie Gillespie. Where might Shake fit in this pantheon? To what extent, if any, does he fit the stereotype of the black jazzman? The classic jazz musician's story is one of ascent — from slavery to freedom, poverty to wealth, immigrant to citizen. Onward and upward.[7] Shake's story, however, does not follow this path.

With a young family to support, his attention was primarily on making a living, and playing music became the obvious solution. Thus, his early musical career was very diverse. It ranged, for example, from appearances as a flamboyant trumpeter in cabaret, to singing bass with a vocal quartet and covering the latest hits by American groups such as the Coasters, on a Saturday night ITV series, *Oh Boy!*, launched in 1958. He obtained early gigs with Mike McKenzie's Harlem All Stars, and further work came courtesy of musician friends from the Caribbean. It was while playing with the All Stars that he met both Coleridge Goode, destined to become a famed bassist, and Joe Harriott, alto sax genius and soon to pioneer free form. It was Goode who suggested he join the Harriott Quintet, which, by 1958, had a regular weekly gig at the Marquee Club at 165 Oxford Street. Nevertheless, he would later claim that on reflection he did not relish the night club gigs which he found 'depressing'.[8] Similarly, his first encounter with an English jazz club was off-putting because of the cramped, seedy and smoky atmosphere.

Oxford Street comprises the northern edge of the Soho rectangle. As well as sex clubs, restaurants and taxi-driver cafes, Soho, in the 1950s and 1960s, hosted after-hour drinking clubs. It was then, when official London night life closed down, that Soho came alive. Officially, these were members only clubs though single night membership was easily arranged. It was a rough-and-tumble space that suited gay or straight, bohemian or well-heeled. It was an atmosphere that Shake learned to relish.

Shake soon discovered the Sunset Club in Carnaby Street as one venue for contacts. In one of his televised reminiscences, many years later, he describes it as located in 'one of the darkest places in Carnaby Street. Another basement location with a lot of puddles of water but its advantage was this was the place I ran into all the black musicians I used to hear about from home — both West Indians and Americans.'[9] An after-hours spot, it was where, after their formal gigs, famous American artists would come to perform.

The Marquee, which was to be found in the basement of the Academy Cinema, was a ballroom which had hosted dance orchestras and big bands during the early 1950s. During much of that decade, however, it was a failing venue until Harold Pendleton, a music business executive, took over its management in 1958 and established regular weekend jazz nights. The first Jazz at the Marquee night was held on 19 April 1958. Decorated like a circus big top with a red and white striped canopy in imitation of a marquee, the venue quickly became a success, hosting a range of regular resident bands including Johnny Dankworth, Chris Barber and the Joe Harriott Quintet. Gene Lawrence, the St Lucian folk/jazz guitarist, attended one weekend in the early 1960s to hear the Harriott Quintet. He remembers it as 'a smoky, dim, crowded room, a heavy atmosphere with many bodies. When Shake and Joe Harriott played I jostled to the front, their performance making it all tolerable.'[10] Tony Gibbs, an engineer and ex-pupil of Shake's at the St Vincent BGS, remembers going regularly to the Marquee around that time. 'When I lived in London in 1962-

Shake with pianist Pat Smythe in the Coach and Horses, Soho, 1960. (*Val Wilmer*)

63, I went to the Marquee Jazz Club almost every Saturday to listen to the Joe Harriott Quintet which included Shake Keane on trumpet and flugelhorn.' He remembers the place as being 'regularly full, but not jam packed; it was a jacket and tie affair and you went to listen to the music rather than dance to it.'[11]

The Quintet also played at the Flamingo, another basement, at 33-37 Wardour Street in London and described in Kenny Wilson's blog as 'a sweaty, smoky, scarlet-walled night club… famous for its weekend all-nighters operating from midnight to six in the morning.'[12] The association with the Marquee also led to the Quintet being in the line-up to play at the first three annual National Jazz Festival weekends, started by Pendleton in 1961, at the Richmond Athletic Ground, in the London suburbs.

During this time — the 1950s — the black popular music scene was also undergoing considerable change, and Shake was in the thick of it. West African musicians had established a foothold in London since the 1940s when Ambrose Adekoya Campbell — acknowledged by Fela Kuti as 'the father of modern Nigerian music' — had established his West African Rhythm Brothers. With Campbell came Nigerian highlife. Though highlife music was played right across West Africa, its place of origin is recognised as Ghana. It grew out of a musical tradition known as *Adaha*,[13] which blended local, Caribbean and European music and included a range of Western instruments and rhythms. Among these was calypso, brought to West Africa by the West India Regiment when it was stationed in the then Gold Coast during the third Anglo-Ashanti War (1873-1874). By the 1920s, a syncretic music had emerged that eventually became known as highlife, taking slightly different forms according to local musical influences. At Ghana's independence in 1957, President Kwame Nkrumah declared highlife the official music of the country.

It was the arrival of many West African and West Indian musicians in London during this period, and the growth of black and nationalist consciousness across the colonised world, that opened the way for further musical crossovers between West Indian and West African musicians and styles. For example, the Sierra Leone calypsonian, Ali (Lord) Ganda, recorded with Trinidadian Rupert Nurse's Calypso Band in London. Shake was very much part of this development, and his adaptability to a range of musical genres served him well. As early as 1954 he had recorded some highlife material for the West Africa market with his own band, *Highlifers*, created for studio work. The band members included Denny Wright, Joe 'Chet' Sampson, Phil Seamen and Shake Keane. Shake later recorded with Ambrose Campbell — playing on some tracks of *High Life Today* (1968), an album where he shared the flugelhorn role with Barbadian Harry Beckett. The record company, Melodisc, supported this cultural interchange by exporting calypso and highlife discs from Britain to West Africa and the Caribbean.

In the 1960s, Shake made several recordings in a more mainstream vein, arranged by bandleaders Johnny Keating and Ivor Raymonde. He was at his most prolific in the years 1962-1964 when he had on release a mixture of some 15 singles, EPs and LPs that included cover versions of popular ballads and compositions in the bossa nova rhythm.

By 1959 Shake's reputation as an accomplished soloist was on the rise. And it was not unusual for him to be in the company of musicians, such as members of the Ellington band, and for him to be invited to sit in and informally jam with them at after-hours clubs when they came through London. The photograph (see page 37) shows him in 1959 with Sonny Stitt and Dizzy Gillespie as they take an informal cigarette break.

Jump forward some 60 years and the blogger, MM, under the byline *Night of the Living Vinyl*, was sufficiently captivated by Shake's output of popular music in the 1960s to offer a review of this material. He unstintingly praises Shake's ability to undertake 'difficult and demanding concepts', and describes his range of playing as 'impeccable'. But he concludes that in the final analysis the records did not sell well enough for him to receive the recognition that he wanted and deserved. MM sums up this phase of Shake's career as, in effect, a glorious failure: 'From ground-breaking jazz to radio friendly covers it must have seemed to Keane that he had tried everything to make it in British jazz. He had played with some of the best musicians that Britain had to offer and he had made four records under his own name. However money was still tight and the name of Shake Keane was still a long way off from being well known'.[14]

This lack of recognition, however, did not apply to the jazz connoisseur, and overlooks the fact that in the 1960s Shake appeared regularly in British jazz magazines and was the focus of regular record release and performance reviews, as well as occasional interviews about the free form music he and others were exploring. His time with the Joe Harriott Quintet excited such interest among jazz aficionados that both Shake's departure to study at university and his return to the Quintet one year later were considered sufficiently newsworthy to be reported in the October 1961 edition of *Jazz News*.

His facility with a range of styles earned him the label of musical 'chameleon' from Michael Garrick, the English jazz composer and band leader. Garrick was especially struck by Shake's magical facility with the horn, which he said was 'like breathing'. His opinion that Shake was more committed to playing as sideman rather than to forming or administering a band of his own is supported by the fact that despite leading his *Highlifers* on record sleeves, on vinyl he appeared most often as featured artist: 'Shake Keane and…' or specialist sideman rather than touring his own band. A prominent characteristic of his playing style, as the jazz historian Val Wilmer notes, is a distinct movement between playfulness and anger — also at times to be seen in his poetry (see Chapters 6/7). As she puts it in a biographical sketch: 'As a trumpeter, Keane's main influences were Dizzy Gillespie and Miles Davis, but by the beginning of the 1960s he had developed an instantly recognisable

Shake with saxophonist Sonny Stitt (left) and trumpeter Dizzy Gillespie (right) during 'Jazz at the Phillharmonic' tour, 1958. (*Val Wilmer*)

style. His playing combines two extremes: the fragile lyricism for which the wide-bore flugelhorn is particularly suited, and an almost brutal aggressiveness and unpredictability. It is this "sound of surprise" in his playing, and his ability to handle music of any kind that puts him at the forefront of his generation of trumpeters.'[15]

The Gillespie/Davis allusion supports Garrick's 'chameleon' observation. While Shake received glowing recognition for his 'featured' appearances, his chameleon characteristic also worked in another way. Uninterested in entering the limelight as a bandleader, his willingness, when called on, to adopt an easy-going style extended to impromptu pub sessions, for example on Sunday afternoons at the

Coleherne, then also known as a gay pub, in South Kensington's Old Brompton Road, where he would play with the pub's resident Russ Henderson's Band. Far from being snobbish about his music he was happy to mix with amateurs as much as with professional musicians.

When Shake's reputation reached its zenith it was not, however, for his versatility but for his mastery of free form jazz with the flugelhorn. In the view of Val Wilmer, it was not until he recorded with Joe Harriott that he had his chance to shine. Commenting on this, Coleridge Goode quotes Val Wilmer and others writing in *The New Grove Dictionary of Jazz* (1988), where his playing is described as 'retain[ing] a singing, shapely sense of melody and (he) soon became recognised as the most accomplished jazz trumpeter of his generation in England.'[16] His son, Roland Ramanan, also an accomplished jazz musician, more precisely identified what made his technique special. He recollected that Shake could hold his own with 'just about anybody… His technique and musical ear, honed by the militaristic training of his father were exceptional. He had a unique style of phrasing that was all his own and highly distinctive, especially on the flugelhorn. Very expressive, it really reflected his puckish sense of humour.'[17]

An appreciation of his artistry was not confined to music critics or family members. For seven successive years (1960-66), jazz polls in *Melody Maker* put Shake on flugelhorn at number one in the Miscellaneous Instruments section, and he was regularly voted high in the polls as a trumpeter. He achieved this pinnacle of recognition partly through his association with two musicians of Jamaican origin: Coleridge Goode, bass player with the Joe Harriott Quintet, and Joe Harriott himself, alto sax player and driven innovator of British free form jazz.

The connection between Shake, Harriott and Goode was Mike

McKenzie's London-based All Stars. McKenzie, originally Oscar Grenville Hastings McKenzie, was a Guyanese pianist and a regular broadcaster with the BBC playing a wide variety of popular styles. Both Coleridge Goode and Joe Harriott had toured with his band in 1953, and Shake got to know them as regular sidemen at that time through this connection. The lynchpin for Shake's development in free form jazz was his contact with Harriott. Five years later he met Harriott again while still working with the BBC. Harriott had been suffering from tuberculosis and was convalescing for an extended period at Pinewood Sanatorium, a specialist hospital in Berkshire. Shake went to interview him for a BBC radio programme he was making. Harriott talked about the new music that he would term 'free form'. It is quite likely that the ideas that Joe discussed with Shake were already grounded in practice. The author and jazz critic Hilary Moore suggests that Harriott's experimentation in free form may have started a few years earlier.[18]

Goode became probably Shake's closest friend in the jazz world. Goode's autobiography, *Bass Lines: A Life in Jazz*, shows clearly how much Shake meant to him. 'Our Caribbean backgrounds drew us close together and we felt the same way about a lot of things... He was my best friend.'[19] Yet the contrast between these two friends could not be greater.

When I met Goode, he was in his seventies. He was a tall wiry black man who had kept himself fit. In contrast with Shake's tendency to periodic rumbustiousness, he had a quiet penetrating gaze behind metal-rimmed spectacles. Along with a facade of English understatement — he described the 6ft 4ins Shake as 'an imposing chap' — he exuded a calm, old-world courtesy. One spring morning we sat in a large, carpeted room at the top of his house in London's Notting Hill, the same house where Shake had lived decades earlier. In the background a reel-to-reel tape recorder played Michael Garrick's J*azz Praises*. The combined voices of the Hastings Girls Choir interspersed with Shake's flugelhorn solos broke the occasional silence. Goode occasionally gave a quiet chuckle, exuding warmth and nostalgia, as he recalled Shake's deep, mellow voice and how he loved to talk.

The two men had much in common: in particular, the experience of migrating from the Caribbean to Britain, and a background that valued self-improvement, as exemplified by their respective fathers. Both fathers were self-educated, with an instinctive ear that served them well in their organisation of choral groups in their respective islands. Both fathers had high expectations of their children. Both Shake and Coleridge were named after famous musicians: Coleridge after Samuel Coleridge Taylor, the composer and conductor with an English mother and Sierra Leonean father; and Shake after James McGranahan, the composer of hymns. Both fathers had ensured their sons had a formal musical upbringing that exposed them to a wide variety of music. They had each received what Derek Walcott called 'a sound colonial education'.[20] The aspirational and somewhat regimented demands of their colonial origins — which pushed many towards the respectable professions — led Coleridge to sum up the weight laid on their shoulders: 'We both had been made to feel that you had to earn your place in society.'[21]

Goode also made some significant interventions in Shake's life in England. First, he persuaded Shake to try the flugelhorn, the instrument with which he became most identified. Goode's imaginative suggestion proved to be a revelation. Shake later claimed that he was responsible for introducing the flugelhorn as a jazz instrument in Europe.[22] In an interview in 1988 towards the end of his career, Shake was asked by Peter Clayton, the BBC radio jazz presenter and critic, what was worth coming to London for? Shake replied: 'It was mostly playing the flugelhorn that was an instrument that I didn't know before. I didn't naturally hear the trumpet in my head...I was searching for that sound...[the flugelhorn] it was the most satisfying sound to me; through the flugelhorn I was able to express myself fully.'[23] The flugelhorn that Shake turned to with such effect is an unusual instrument, to be found neither in a jazz nor popular band at that time. It is the same length as the trumpet but has a wider conical bore and a deeper, funnel-like mouthpiece. Much mellower in tone than the trumpet, with which Shake was first associated, it has a poignancy that can be both bitter and sweet, an expressive range from anger to gentleness. For a while, finding the right mouthpiece was a problem, until Shake adapted one from a trumpet, and later had a special mouthpiece made.[24]

Goode's second intervention was that, having heard Shake play, he recommended to Joe Harriott that Shake should join the group, following the departure of Hank Shaw, the Quintet's original trumpeter, who was not enthusiastic about the new direction that the Quintet was taking. This was around the time that the band was starting to rehearse their experiments in free form. Shake was then aged 32. With Goode's encouragement, in 1960, Harriott invited Shake to join the band for a trial period, and, very soon, a firm link, a willingness to be fully absorbed into Harriott's free form musical experiment, was established. Shake would remain a fixture in the Quintet until 1964.

Although there was some unity between Shake and Harriott, especially as black outsiders in Britain, a word picture of Harriott by Shake brings out their contrasting characteristics. As an ex-teacher and poet, Shake had a linguistic precision that his fellow musician lacked. He described how, 'Joe had a way of going roundabout this, that or the other. He would say, for example, "I would play something and you would 'overshadow' me." By overshadow he meant counterpoint. It took a little while for me to understand Joe's personal vocabulary.'[25] He also drew attention to Harriott's single-mindedness, essentially living for his music, in this way: 'It would have been difficult to imagine Joe spending his last years… having kids around him, friendly conversation, what not. I imagine that at the end he was thinking what he would do next on the saxophone regardless of who said yes or no.'[26]

Shake and Harriott were very different personalities, the former often convivial, easy-going and light-hearted, the latter taciturn and driven. In a televised interview, Shake observed the contradictory combination that was Harriott: 'Very fragile and tender and very aggressive — as if he was trying to prove himself — which of course he had to do in real life… a stimulating person musically but a very irritating man otherwise.'[27] But Shake proved to be the partner who brought out the best in Joe Harriott's music.

What was the musical revolution that Harriott was spearheading? Harriott's quintet of highly talented individuals — Harriott (alto sax), Shake (flugelhorn), Coleridge Goode (double bass), Pat Smythe (piano) and Phil Seamen (drums) — became, according to Coleridge, the most controversial group on the London jazz scene of the 1960s. New ideas from the United States about rhythm and harmony in jazz were in circulation; at the same time, Joe Harriott was developing and refining his own ideas. He described his initiative as an opportunity for musicians to paint abstract pictures in sound. Shake's description of Harriott's intervention in free form is as good a definition as any: 'Jazz solos are usually based on chords. He began to think if you could get away from the chords and solo as free as possible. The other frontline men have to listen and jump in if he feels he can…it's a question of pooling life experience of music and putting them

LONDON IS THE PLACE FOR ME

Joe Harriott Quintet at National Jazz Festival, Richmond, Surrey, 1963. L to R, Pat Smythe (not seen, piano), Bobby Orr (drums), Joe Harriott (alto sax), Coleridge Goode (bass), Shake Keane (trumpet). (*Val Wilmer*)

together.'[28] As he went on to point out, people often make the mistake of latching on to 'free' and forget 'form'. In other words the musician doesn't simply play wildly; it is more that one is free to create musical form 'as it happens'. Shake argued that it was Harriott's genius to conceive of this. He wrote distinctive introductory themes that were open enough for members of the Quintet to take up the lead as the mood took them, while being responsive to the other band members.

And so each musician had to be able to perform as the music dictated, catching the mood of the band member who had taken the instrumental lead at any given moment. This required each of them to have considerable musical knowledge on which to draw. Harriott's themes provided the opportunity for the band members to 'change the forms as we saw fit.'[29] The resulting harmonies and musical relationships flowed out of free interaction between the musicians. What this required of the audience was a willingness to engage with these new harmonies.

Of course, if handled poorly this could be a recipe for musical chaos, and there were plenty of naysayers ready to skewer the experiment when they found the jump to free or new harmonious expression beyond them. In the early days when the band showcased experimentation, one reviewer expressed just such reservations. Under a banner headline 'Abstraction or Distraction' in *Jazz News*, Daniel Halperin first critiqued the term 'free form', questioning 'how something which has 'form' can strictly speaking be considered 'free'. He was similarly upset by the linking of 'abstract' to the notion of 'composed', as in the term 'abstract composition'. He went on to describe one performance of the Quintet as: 'a series of sounds… (similar to)… the woolly din of a bunch of sick sheep squealing through a quagmire in a hail storm.'[30] But beyond such disdain, there was also a growing interest in and excitement about these musical developments. Some months later, Kitty Grime, in a review of the Harriott Quintet at Ronnie Scott's Club for the same magazine, described the playing as 'complex but with a very direct appeal, put over with a high seriousness that compels respect.'[31]

Two obvious but important features of the Quintet were that it was all male and racially and culturally diverse. It comprised two black Jamaicans, a black Vincentian and two white British members (English and Scottish). Does this matter? It matters artistically because for the group to function effectively a high level of interdependence and understanding was required. The group had to know and trust each other. In an interview with Kitty Grime in 1962, Shake emphasised the importance of the personal relationships among the musicians and of the mood of the lead individual and the event itself: 'We usually have a rhythmic pulse or pattern going... I might be playing something soulful, and then Joe can get intense, so you have a conflict. Or he might join me and you get a sympathy. The music draws its strength from this sympathy or contrast, and the vigour with which each man makes his contribution...The biggest freedom in our music is that... the standard is an emotional one. When you're playing you're listening, not to the chords as in conventional jazz, but to Pat or Phil or Cole or Joe — and you have to *know* that man, and how he's feeling on the particular night and that particular moment in the set to try and feel how he is likely to behave.'[32] The response or movement in the work between one musician and another might be sympathetic or rebellious, but it relied on trust.

Another feature of the group was that its membership comprised strong and distinctive characters. Seamen was a highly regarded drummer who had previously played with Shake's *Highlifers* and was continually in demand. He enjoyed being contradictory and getting under Harriott's skin. Shake, too, had a contrary relationship with

Harriott. While they were musically compatible and aligned, off stage there were divisions. Himself formally educated, he saw Harriott as stubborn and inarticulate. Reminiscing years later, Shake explained, with an older man's ironic inflection around the word 'deep': 'We argued a lot about deep philosophical things of which I felt he didn't have a full grasp.'[33] In contrast to Harriott, Shake gained the reputation of being an easy-going but likeable and articulate rogue. For example, as an apparent gesture of friendship and when playing in other bands, though his necktie was often the scrawniest and least desirable, he would often offer to exchange his own for that of another musician. Smythe and Goode appear to have been the more steadying influences in the band.

Shake was well aware of the extent of their innovative work. In an interview in 1973 with Canute James in *Melody Maker,* he made the claim that, 'We were the first to play free form music in London… I have a feeling we were playing free form a little before Ornette Coleman — our thing predates his.'[34] In a later interview in 1995 he remained adamant that, 'We did ours independently… not similarly.'[35] Many now recognise Joe Harriott as the pioneer of free form in Britain. Though it took a long time for this recognition to dawn, it has been aided by a growing body of literature recollecting Harriott's work, helped in particular by Alan Robertson's 2003 biography, *Joe Harriott: Fire in His Soul.* Then, in 2007 Hilary Moore devoted a chapter of his *Inside British Jazz: Crossing Borders of Race, Nation and Class* to assessing the role and impact of the Joe Harriott Quintet in jazz circles. The autobiographies of Coleridge Goode and Michael Garrick also draw attention to the Quintet's achievements. Why did it take so long for the recognition to dawn?

Wider cultural issues of the time may well have impeded recognition of the innovative role of the Quintet. The historian Eric

Hobsbawm, who reviewed and reported on jazz throughout the 1950s and 1960s, argued, along with others, that, as the 1960s wore on, the jazz scene faced a severe challenge in terms of social and cultural change. In essence, rock music increasingly deprived jazz of its audience.[36] And it's also worth observing that in struggling to obtain recognition any major change to an established form encounters gatekeepers, critics who for various reasons are wary of innovation. It takes time for an audience to develop a feeling for the sounds and harmonies of a new music. This time-lag can often be to the disadvantage of the innovator.

Goode claimed that, at the time, race was a factor in the muted critical response to Harriott's free form innovations. He put it like this: 'In the end, unfortunately, one puts it down to the fact that Joe wasn't a white Englishman. Had he been one, things would've been different. There can be no other explanation.' Roland Ramanan also suggests that racism may have limited the recognition that Shake, too, was due. Ramanan interpreted his father's sideman role as not so much a matter of choice as of circumstances. He observed: 'Shake never became a musical leader or someone who developed the group or recordings under his own name but that is hardly surprising given the forces stacked against him at the time. Jazz is full of brilliant players who didn't make their mark as they might have.'[37]

Generally, the black Caribbean migrant experience of the late 1940s and 1950s, as is well documented, went beyond the cold shoulder that most immigrants experience. Despite the demand for employment in low-level essential services that Caribbean migrants invariably filled, housing and employment discrimination remained rife and the social stigma associated with a black skin was commonplace. However, racism, both institutionally and personally, is not always simple to categorise at the individual level. In Shake's case, he was a protean artistic intellectual whose individual skill and outward-going personality were in demand and he quickly became popular. How did Shake respond to racism? It appears that for his part he played down the experience of individual racism. A regular pub goer, he encountered white antipathy early on, but his attitude was that by persevering and going back regularly the white locals would adjust to the black presence. He also chose to ridicule rather than aggressively oppose such attitudes. Alan Robertson, recounts a telephone conversation he had about Shake with the white baritone saxophonist player, Harry Klein, who temporarily deputised in the all-black Mike McKenzie band. Apparently Shake asked the recruit, 'Aren't you scared we might eat you?'[38]

Music was one area where black artists did find a measure of acceptance. Shake recounted how the multiracial Quintet regularly played to predominantly white middle-class audiences. He observed: 'In the five years that I worked at the Marquee club very few working-class people came to the sessions… I counted nine West Indians and most of them came to see me because they knew me at home, not to listen to jazz.'[39] Ironically, then, it seems that in 1960s Britain, without a predominantly white audience, the Quintet would have had a more muted response given the background of the punters turning up in the clubs to listen to their music.[40] At the same time, the trust and commitment demanded of each member of the Quintet, especially when they played free form, was testimony to a musical form that, without elaborate fanfare, bridged the racial divide.

For the years that Shake was with the Quintet, the group stuck to their principles, regularly incorporating free form pieces in their repertoire. As sideman, Shake contributed to six albums by the Joe Harriott Quintet. First was *Southern Horizons* (1960), then *Free Form* (1960) presented the original musical ideas, followed by *A Guy Called*

Joe (EP, 1961), *Abstract* (1963), *Movement* (1964) and *High Spirits* (released 1965) offering further musical explorations. Some critics heralded them as innovative or even revolutionary.[41] But as innovative as the work was, it didn't pay the bills.

Ultimately most bands break up and the Quintet was no exception. One practical problem for Shake was that work opportunities started to fall off. For a time they played three nights per week, Friday, Saturday and Sunday. The arrangement was first cut to two nights then one. As he observed: 'I can't live on one gig a week'.[42] It is also often difficult to maintain the high levels of trust that such innovative music-making demands.

And so the combination of a reduced number of regular weekend gigs and the lure of a fully paid, three-year contract with the Kurt Edelhagen Orchestra in Europe were major incentives for Shake to leave the Joe Harriott Quintet. Shake's departure was a considerable loss to the band. Though a variety of replacements were tried for a year, until Kenny Wheeler became Shake's regular replacement in the Quintet in 1967, it proved difficult for Harriott to find a comparable musician to act as a regular counterpoint to his own playing. It was Coleridge Goode's view that it was Shake's departure for Germany in 1965 that had led, in effect, to the Quintet's demise.[43]

Notes

1 Nanton, "*Travels*."
2 Austin, interview.
3 Nancy Foner, "Gender and Migration: West Indians in Comparative Perspective," *International Migration* 47, no.1 (2009): 1, https://doi.org/10.1111/j.1468-2435.2008.00480.x accessed May 2019.
4 Pixley, "Musicians of the Caribbean," 35.
5 Anthony Harkavy, email to author, May 30, 2020. Jeremy Robson kindly enabled contact with Anthony Harkavy.
6 Cyrus, interview.

7   For a contrasting perspective on a jazz musician's life see Geoff Dyer, *But Beautiful: A Book About Jazz* (New York: North Point Press, 1991).
8   James, "Shake Keane All Over."
9   Rhythms of the World, *Shake, Beat and Dub*, directed by Mary Dickinson, BBC TV (Arena), July 4, 1992.
10 Gene Lawrence, email correspondence with author, March 31, 2020.
11 Tony Gibbs, email correspondence with author, April 13, 2020.
12 Kenny Wilson, "Live music clubs and coffee bars in Soho, London in the 1950s and 60s," https://kennywilson.org/2016/07/21/live-music-clubs-and-coffee-bars-in-soho-london-in-the-1950s-and-60s/, accessed April 2020.
13 Micah Motenko, "Highlife in the Ghanaian Music Scene: A Historical and Socio-Political Perspective", 2011, Independent Study Project (ISP) Collection 1107, https://digitalcollections.sit.edu/isp_collection/1107, accessed August 2020.
14 MM, "Night of the Living Vinyl," http://nightofthelivingvinyl.blogspot.com/2011/03/, accessed May 20, 2019.
15 Wilmer, "Keane," 2004.
16 Coleridge Goode and Roger Cotterrell, *Bass Lines: A Life in Jazz* (Miami: Parkwest Publications, 1999), chapter 8, para 12, Kindle.
17 Roland Ramanan, email correspondence with author, March 8, 2020.
18 Hilary Moore, *Inside British Jazz: Crossing Borders of Race, Nation and Class* (London: Routledge, 2007), 71.
19 Goode and Cotterrell, *Bass Lines*, chapter 8, para 16, Kindle.
20 Derek Walcott, *Derek Walcott - Collected Poems 1948-1984* (London: Faber & Faber, 1992), 346.
21 Goode and Cotterrell, *Bass Lines*, chapter 9, para 29, Kindle.
22 Personalities Caribbean: *The International Guide to Who's Who in the West Indies, Bahamas and Bermuda*, 1977-1978, 6th Edition (Kingston: Personalities Ltd), 807.
23 Shake Keane, interview with Peter Clayton, *Sounds of Jazz*, BBC radio, December 10, 1988.
24 Larry Brown Jr, a fellow trumpeter who knew Shake in Germany, remembered that he played a Couesnon flugelhorn.
25 Alan Robertson, *Joe Harriott: Fire in His Soul* (London: Northway, 2011), 55.
26 Robertson, *Joe Harriott,* 209-10.
27 *Shake, Beat and Dub*, BBC TV, 1992
28 Austin, interview.
29 Austin, interview.
30 Daniel Halperin, "Abstraction or Distraction," *Jazz News*, 5, no.6, February 11, 1961, 2.
31 Kitty Grime, "Joe Harriott Quintet at Ronnie Scotts," *Jazz News*, 5, no.38, September 20, 1961, 10.
32 Kitty Grime, "Star Sideman: Shake Keane talks to Kitty Grime," *Jazz News,* 6, no.5, January 31, 1962, 9.
33 *Shake, Beat and Dub*, BBC TV, 1992.
    "*Shake Keane All Over*"
34 James, Shake Keane All Over.
35 Austin, interview.

36 Eric Hobsbawm, *The Jazz Scene* (London: Faber and Faber, 1992).
37 Ramanan, email correspondence.
38 Robertson, *Fire in His Soul*, 65.
39 *Shake, Beat and Dub*, BBC TV, 1992.
40 Jazz, especially modern jazz, has not been a prominent part of Caribbean culture. The many 'jazz' festivals that the region has hosted over the years quickly embraced a range of musical genres.
41 Shake was less sanguine about such claims. In later life he reflected: 'Personally I don't like theories about jazz and development. All the jazz musicians I talked to in America are really jazz politicians, they keep having theories and trying to relate jazz to social conditions .....But I don't think that is the main focus.' Shake Keane, "Held Together With Rhythm and Rhymes", *Caribbean Perspective*, no.46-47, January-March 1990, 22.
42 Austin, interview.
43 In 1972, drummer Phil Seamen died, aged 46, from a drug overdose. In 1973, Joe Harriott died, aged 44, his genius essentially under-recognised. Pat Smythe, the group's pianist, died in 1983.

Shake collaborated with composer Michael Garrick in innovative work combining jazz and poetry. Here, photographed at Theatre Royal, Stratford East, London, 1965. (*Courtesy Jeremy Robson*)

4 / MOVING ON

Another significant high point in Shake's London career in jazz was his association with the composer and band leader, Michael Garrick. This connection resulted in further musical exploration, this time combining jazz and poetry,[1] and jazz and religious music. Shake had first got to know Michael Garrick while they were students at London University. The link was solidified at the Marquee where Garrick also played and Shake would appear as a guest star with Garrick's Quartet. In appearance, Garrick — a short, white, slightly built Englishman with a neat goatee beard — was the opposite of Shake, but they had a mutual interest in philosophy and religion. In his autobiography, *Dusk Fire: Jazz in English Hands*, Garrick explains how his religious and mystical interests developed — in particular the effect of attending a Theosophical Society retreat in 1962. Shake had a background in Methodism and had published two essays exploring the spiritual element in contemporary Caribbean poetry in *Bim* (see Chapter 6).

As jazz musicians Garrick and Shake also shared an interest in innovation, in their case linking jazz to poetry, and developing a jazz format for sacred music. Shake initiated ideas for a few of the tracks they recorded and this cemented their working relationship. In combining jazz with poetry, Garrick, a pianist, composer, arranger and innovator, aimed to bring together the two artistic forms with a view to enhancing both. Garrick saw at once that Joe Harriott and Shake were, in his words 'in a different league' from most other musicians he knew. He was drawn to Shake's instinctive feel for music and his knowledge of how to phrase a piece by turning the volume up or down. So he jumped at the opportunity to work with them.

In June 1961, two jazz and poetry events took place in London's Royal Festival Hall. The first event was organised by the poet and (later publisher) Jeremy Robson in the main auditorium and the other, a few days later, by Michael Garrick in the smaller Recital Room. Whereas Garrick's event featured readers from London University, the readings organised by Robson were by the poets themselves, reading their own work, a format that would continue. Garrick and Robson's events had in common the idea of bringing the two artistic forms together with a view to enhancing both. Robson attended Garrick's event and they soon teamed up.

The novelty of combining poetry and jazz quickly grew in popularity and with Robson's creative programming, and the inclusion of many leading poets to read alongside a great jazz line-up, the ensemble of poets and musicians soon began to fill venues around the country. Both poets and musicians enjoyed the relaxed informality not usually associated with poetry readings. Audiences ranged in size for these events from around 500 to 3,000. Over the next decade some 300 jazz and poetry concerts took place in theatres, town halls, universities, festivals and clubs. The popularity of the form also led to regional TV and BBC Third Programme broadcasts.

Shake's involvement began in February 1962, with the third of these concerts which was held at the Belgrade Theatre, Coventry. Garrick's regular quartet for the live performance of poetry and jazz events comprised Garrick on piano, Johnny Taylor on bass, Colin Barnes on drums and Shake on trumpet and flugelhorn. Coleridge Goode joined later and occasionally Joe Harriott was also part of the mix. Shake's easy-going, extrovert nature made him, according to Robson, 'an extremely popular regular', and, by the time of his move to Germany in 1965, he had participated in some 40 jazz and poetry concerts. Although Shake was a serious and dedicated musician, he was willing and able to respond to innovation and impromptu moments.

Robson recollected the following story: 'In the Argo recording[1] of a concert we gave in the famous Abbey Road studios before a live audience, the tape snapped and we had to halt the proceedings for a few minutes. "Let's play something while we wait," Shake suggested. "How about 'Jada'?" I said… away they went in true Dixieland style, Shake leading, and Garrick, Joe Harriott and the others following. A couple of thrilling moments of real joy. They kept it on the final record.'[2]

Some of the collaboration was captured on an early EP recording 'Blues for the Lonely' on which Robson reads four of his poems to Michael Garrick's setting. The exception was the title poem, which Robson had written to the 'Blue in Green' track on Miles Davis' *Kind of Blue*.[3] Here Shake plays with a brilliance and sensitivity that even Davis might have applauded.

The poets that Shake gravitated to at these events included Jeremy Robson, Dannie Abse, Laurie Lee, John Smith, Ted Hughes and Spike Milligan. He particularly enjoyed the latter's idiosyncratic and irreverent humour, and Shake's later writing, particularly *One A Week With Water*, reflects some of this irreverence (see Chapter 7). Robson recollects that Milligan, who also played the trumpet, was always

Spike Milligan with Shake in the
background at a jazz and poetry event.
(*Courtesy Jeremy Robson*)

riveted by Shake's dynamic playing and presence. In the context of the mixed milieu of poetry and jazz, the online music critic and blogger MM has noted the irony of Shake contributing to jazz and poetry only through his music-making. This led him to wonder: 'What did Shake think about the poets he accompanied? Did he ever want to put his trumpet down and read some of his verse? And why did no one ask him'.[4] James Mitchell distinctly remembers attending at least one event at which Shake contributed by reading his verse.[5] But beyond this recollection, there is no evidence that he was ever asked to read his own poetry at these public performances.

When asked about this, Robson's comment bears out this observation: 'I don't recall Shake ever reading a poem of his own — I'm not sure we were aware he wrote poetry seriously or we would surely have asked him to read. He never mentioned it but was very responsive to the poetry read and always played a solo number after

Laurie Lee's lyrical reading that often concluded with "She's Like a Swallow".[6] Similarly, in Shake's 1995 interview with David Austin, he states that although he was a reader and contributor to *Caribbean Voices*, 'in England no one knew what I did in poetry' and, more decisively he added, 'I made no attempt to get into the poetry scene in England.' However, I imagine that he would surely have been aware of the irony of playing for other poets. Perhaps he simply settled for the musician's role, yet, despite the informal nature of the setting, it's a reflection of how easily a musician is pigeonholed in metropolitan society.

These concerts certainly widened the circle of artists with whom Shake worked. Christiane remembers that they occasionally attended what she called 'bohemian parties' in Hampstead with a number of these poets. But she observed that Shake felt sidelined and uncomfortable in such circles. He was more at home, she felt, with an intellectual West Indian crowd that included students like his boyhood friend Son Mitchell, John Compton of St Lucia, later the island's Prime Minister, and the Barbadian Oliver Jackman, who would become a diplomat. Mitchell was often the host of such gatherings in his north London flat on the Finchley Road. The Marxist thinker CLR James, also a friend of Mitchell, regularly attended.

The first concert of *Jazz Praises*, combining sacred music and jazz, was held at St Michael the Archangel, Aldershot, on 2 November 1967. In these concerts Garrick was committed to expressing what he called 'deep profound experiences' through his music-making. And so he combined choral work with jazz. The aim, as he described it, was 'to combine jazz fire with the formal and sublime, not forever keeping them apart'. A sleeve note, written in 1965 by Garrick for an original EP titled *Anthem*, captures the innovation by and collaboration in sacred music of these two musicians. Garrick wrote on the EP sleeve note: '*Anthem* developed on a suggestion of Shake Keane, from a phrase occurring in 'A Face in the Crowd,' a free form jazz setting for a poem by Jeremy Robson. It has a scalar skeleton of C, B flat, A flat, G flat, F, E flat, D, and C which is retained throughout. The dramatic function of the piece is to celebrate Christ's overcoming of death, the horns in the jazz passage focusing on the awakening in the tomb and the rolling of the stone from the door, the chorus summarising the event as it affects humanity.'

By the time of the first *Jazz Praises* concerts, Shake would have left London, but he would occasionally return to play with the Michael Garrick Quintet. He was, for example, 'featured soloist' at St Paul's Cathedral in October 1968, and again at the Martin Luther King memorial concert at Central Hall, Westminster, in 1989.

Again, while this work was stimulating it was not lucrative, so when a better offer came from Germany, Shake accepted. By 1965 he had become known and respected on the touring circuit. For example, he found regular session work with Johnny Keating and His Orchestra. Keating was a well-known composer and arranger for pop stars of the day such as Adam Faith and Petula Clarke. His big band played smooth jazz numbers. Shake was one of seven trumpeters employed in the band.

Shake's playing had first come to the attention of the German big band leader Kurt Edelhagen while Shake was touring in Europe with the Quintet. Edelhagen, who prided himself on the international make up of his orchestra, asked Shake to join his Radio Orchestra at Westdeutscher Radiofunk in Cologne, with a regular salary and an initial contract for three years. Shake moved to Cologne in April 1965 and stayed with the Orchestra for seven years. Financially, these were perhaps his best years.

Left to right: Shake, Jeremy Robson and Joe Harriott outside the Old Vic, London, 1962, on the film set of Young Europe. (*Courtesy Jeremy Robson*)

In Ramanan's view the move to Germany was positive: 'When he moved to Germany… he really had a golden age in terms of his career.'[7] Shake also talked up his experience of playing in big bands: 'I find big bands very stimulating. If you're soloing in a quintet it's exciting but small in terms of volume and intricacy. But in a big band you have the three sections, saxes, trombones and trumpets, and the rhythm section behind you — and it's a marvellous feeling when what you're doing is fitting in with what 15 other people are doing.'[8] But beyond these scraps of information, little is known about his experience of living, working and touring while he was based in Germany. There is one photograph of Shake on tour in Egypt from this time (probably Cairo). His entry in the 1977-78 *Personalities Caribbean Handbook* indicates that he spoke both French and German; given his flair for languages, it seems likely he would have learned German while living there. His *Collected Poems* suggest that a few poems, including the short folk play *Nancitori With Drums*, dated August 1972, were also composed in Cologne.[9]

A small but revealing rebellious moment in a YouTube video is therefore all the more precious. Shot in 1965, the footage captured the Edelhagen Orchestra playing at the Lucerna Palace during the Prague International Jazz Festival. The music critic, Steven Cerra, in his 2013 *Jazz Profiles* blog on the Kurt Edelhagen Orchestra recounts that Edelhagen was called 'Prussian' for his 'rehearsal discipline and severity with players.'[10] The parallel with Shake's disciplined father in his early days of learning to play the trumpet is ironic. Christiane also remarked to me once that she wondered often to what extent Shake's more casual style and spontaneity were subdued or in conflict with Edelhagen's disciplinary demands.

The Orchestra's line-up for this event comprised four trumpets, four trombones, piano, drums and double bass, with Edelhagen conducting. Edelhagen's goal was to make his Orchestra as renowned as that of Stan Kenton, the American band leader he most admired. On tour the orchestra played 'concert jazz'; players, as usual at the time, were all men, dressed in formal black suits, white shirts and bow ties. Two members were black. The brass players are arranged in conventional format with saxophones at the front and trombones and trumpets at the rear. Double bass, piano and drums are to one side. The first piece in the recording is composed by the band member and saxophonist Wilton 'Bogey' Gaynair (who, like Joe Harriott, was a

Shake in rehearsal with the Kurt Edelhagen Orchestra, Cologne. (*Michael Ward/ courtesy Christiane Keane*)

product of the famous Jamaican Alpha Boys' School). At the end of the piece the audience applaud enthusiastically. Each soloist is then named by Edelhagen and prompted to stand and acknowledge the applause. For no more than a few seconds, Shake, the first to be called, breaks the studied decorum. As he sits down with a wide smile he turns his trumpet with the mouthpiece away from him; holding the instrument like a machine gun he rakes it quickly to and fro across the well-dressed audience, offering perhaps mimed notes instead of bullets. In the context of the formality of the occasion, the spontaneous action signals to the audience (and viewers quick enough to spot it) that he won't be subdued or go peacefully into musical regimentation.[11]

SHAKE KEANE
Flügelhorn Soloist-Orchester Edelhagen
KÖLN, Brüsseler Str. 30 · Tel. 24 68 65

Shake's German 'business' card.

Shake left Edelhagen's band in 1972 just before Edelhagen's contract with Westdeutscher Radiofunk came to an end. While based in Germany he also had spells playing in France, Belgium and Switzerland with a range of bands and band leaders including the prestigious Kenny Clarke/Francy Boland Big Band. Shake, by now a well-established soloist fitted easily into the grouping of international talent led by Belgian pianist, composer and arranger Boland and the African-American Clarke, the father of modern jazz drumming. Shake's discography reveals that while based in Cologne he contributed to 17 studio recordings with band leaders as varied as Charly Antolini, Oskar Gottlieb Blarr, Jonny Teupen and Peter Trunk.

Along with his big band commitments Shake also performed as solo guest artist in jazz clubs around Germany. These appearances could be booked at short notice. One such appearance was recounted by Larry Brown Jr (aka Blue Brown), a one-time trumpet player from the United States stationed in Germany at the time. He remembered that in late 1969, Shake appeared at the Jazzgalerie Club in Berlin. Dressed in fringed suede leather he joined the house band already on stage. Brown was won over by Shake's virtuosity and the selflessness of his playing, the way that he allowed other band members to 'stretch out' on their solos. The experience won Brown over to the flugelhorn. In his words: 'Shake's playing informed me that having a unique sound on trumpet is one thing. But the flugelhorn becomes Your Voice!'[12]

One form of moving on, then, was his association with different bands in different countries in Europe. But moving on also took the form of different relationships with women. He had met Christiane Ricard, from Lyon, in 1953 when she went with friends to a London nightclub where Shake was playing. Christiane was at that time a student nurse, but later established a career as a librarian at the Commonwealth Institute in London. This was a time of severe racial tension in London when accommodation was difficult to come by for a black West Indian, with or without a white French wife. They initially lived in what Christiane described as a 'tenement house' in Tufnell Park, then a rundown part of north London. Their landlord was sympathetic to accommodating West Indians. Even so, living conditions were difficult: 'At the time we were all penniless, sleeping in front of paraffin heaters or coal fires.'[13]

By the early 1960s, Shake, Christiane and the two children, Alan, and Noel Julian, who was born in 1962, had moved to Notting Hill, an area of west London with a substantial West Indian population. The Keane family found accommodation in the house of his friend Coleridge Goode, where they lived until Shake left for Germany. But Shake's relationship with Christiane had, by then, begun to fracture. There were various causes of tension. Living in close proximity to

Shake, Goode noticed the contradiction of a powerful personality with a lack of self control, when he had had too much to drink. The drinking may have been symptomatic of a number of frustrations, but in later years Christiane summed up his character in the phrase 'a difficult and provocative man'.[14]

Roland Ramanan suggests that some of this frustration was taken out on Alan. Roland observed simply: 'I was lucky (and so was Julian) in that I escaped the physical and psychological abuse that led to Alan's addiction.'[15] It was severe enough for Christiane to later have only limited contact with Alan who suffered from drug dependency. Christiane was also to experience Shake's anger. She described the break-up of their relationship and ultimate divorce as 'super vitriolic'. Even so, she remained a loyal supporter and followed his career throughout. In later life they had a measure of rapprochement and she received periodic visits from him throughout the 1990s whenever he passed through London.[16] After he died, Christiane, who herself died on 20 March 2005, told Son Mitchell in a letter: 'He was the most important influence in my life.' [17]

One probable reason for the break-up of his marriage to Christiane was that Shake had started a relationship with Elizabeth Uma Ramanan, a Scottish-born woman who had lived for some time in India. Their son, Roland, was born in 1966. According to Roland, Elizabeth met Shake at an extramural study class on jazz. 'She wanted to find out more about the music, expand her horizons and was hooked by the music. Shake described her as "that rare thing; an understanding woman". Roland went on to observe: 'And she had to be. Before I was born, Shake had left for Germany and she had to cope as a single mother working as a manicurist. But my mother was never bitter in the slightest, she absolutely accepted Shake as he was and wasn't.'[18]

Christiane Keane, Shake's first wife. (*Courtesy Laurence Keane*)

In 2001, Christiane held a small lunch party in the family home in Notting Hill to celebrate a BBC Radio 3 programme about Shake called *Angel Horn* I had recently finished making. Both Roland and Julian, and his family were there. During the meal I mentioned to Julian that since his death Shake had become something of a 'hero' in St Vincent because of his international reputation. Julian responded directly that while Shake might be a 'hero' in St Vincent, as a son growing up in a single-parent family he saw him more as a father who abandoned his family when he was needed and certainly not in the light of 'hero'.[19]

Roland Ramanan makes a similar point. 'I rarely saw my father after he left the UK. I have a few hazy memories of fleeting visits in the middle of the night as a child. I only properly got to know him in the early 1990s when he started to come to London more for projects and concerts.' The distance between them was reinforced by the fact that though his mother encouraged Roland to write to Shake, 'He almost never replied… I will always love and respect his playing and his poetry, it has been a part of my upbringing and a part of me. Over the years my view has shifted from one of an absent hero to an absent father.'[20]

By the early 1970s Shake admitted to Michael Garrick that he had seen enough of recording studios and was weary of the rigours of touring. He stated simply that he was 'all played out'. In retrospect, it's a hint that he may have been looking for fulfilment away from music. This something else turned up in the shape of an invitation to join the organising committee of the first CARIFESTA (regional Caribbean Festival of Arts) to be held in Guyana in 1972. The festival had been the idea of Prime Minister Forbes Burnham of Guyana following two successful writers' conventions held there in 1966 and in 1970. This first festival, whose goal is and always has been to encourage Caribbean integration, was hailed as a success, attracting more than 1,000 artists in the fields of music, dance, drama, fine art, folk art, photography and literature, chosen and funded by their governments, from 30 Caribbean and South American countries.[21]

In his twenties Shake had been a strong supporter of Caribbean federation, and for the closing ceremony of the first CARIFESTA, he was inspired to write and read a specially composed poem that offered an idealised and romanticised notion of the region. His poem, a paean to regional unity, brought together the Carib Creator God, Makunaima (literally translates as 'He Works By Night', so one who is never seen), and obversely the Carib devil, as well as wind, mountain and stars. The heady festival experiences may well have helped fuel his appetite for a return to St Vincent. A sense of nostalgia and homesickness is also suggested by six poems about St Vincent which he wrote in London between 1970 and 1972. In *Coming Back*, for example, reading 'she' as a reference to his island, the last stanza offers a strong hint:

Harriott and Shake, with Jeremy Robson in foreground, rehearsing at Robson's home, London, 1965. (*Courtesy Jeremy Robson*)

That year much later
clusters of shining in wet sand
she secretly waited
    should I come surging back old nails
and pride shivering in my belly it really feels
a little like power something like love.[22]

But on a personal level, there may have been other reasons that encouraged departure. The disintegration of his marriage to Christiane and his relationship with Elizabeth Ramanan, each involving child-care responsibilities, were further complicated by a third relationship, which had begun before he left for Europe to join the Kurt Edelhagen Orchestra. This relationship was with Muriel Pick, widely known as Lou, a literature teacher at a secondary school in London and an active socialist. Following his divorce from Christiane, they were married on 10 June 1968 in London.

His return to St Vincent was cemented by the offer of a job in 1973, as Director of Culture, by Son Mitchell, the island's new Premier. There is some uncertainty how this offer was initiated. Kenneth John, the Vincentian journalist and lawyer, suggests that the Education Forum of the People, an unofficial radical group associated with the University of the West Indies Extra-Mural Department in St Vincent, recommended to Mitchell that Shake be offered the position.[23] Shake stated unequivocally that he himself put the idea to the Mitchell-led government.[24] Mitchell claims simply that he brought him back to head the post.[25] Whatever the case, he took up the job and in 1973 he returned home, with Lou. Here, then, was the working out of the returning migrant's dilemma writ large — the offer of service 'back home' or self-fulfilment through music in the adopted country.

Notes

1. "Poetry and Jazz in Concert," Dannie Abse, Laurie Lee, Adrian Mitchell, Jeremy Robson, Michael Garrick Quintet featuring Joe Harriott and Shake Keane. Double LP, Argo, London, 1964.
2. Jeremy Robson, email correspondence with author, May 31, 2020.
3. Michael Garrick with Trevor Bannister, *Dusk Fire: Jazz in English Hands* (Reading: Springdale Publishing, 2010); Jeremy Robson, *Under Cover: A Poet's Life in Publishing...And All That Jazz* (Hull: Biteback Publishing, 2018).
4. MM, "Shake Keane - An Angel Horn - His Solo Albums," 2011,

http://nightofthelivingvinyl.blogspot.com/2011/03/shake-keane.html accessed April 2019.
5. James Mitchell, interview with author, Bequia, St Vincent & the Grenadines, 2020.
6. Robson, email correspondence with author, May 31, 2020.
7. Ramanan, email correspondence, 2020.
8. James, "*Shake Keane All Over.*"
9. The play was performed in 1979 by Shake as a one-man show at St Vincent's Lyric Theatre (cinema) in Kingstown.
10. Steven Cerra, "Orchester Kurt Edelhagen," http://jazzprofiles.blogspot.com/2013/07/orchester-kurt-edelhagen.html, accessed March 2020.
11. International Jazz Festival, Prague, 1965, https://www.youtube.com/watch?v=l3giNP4-V7Q, accessed April 2019.
12. Larry Brown Jr, email correspondence with author, July 16, 2020.
13. Christiane Keane, interview with author, London, 2001.
14. Christiane Keane, letter to James Mitchell, December 1999.
15. Ramanan, email correspondence, 2020.
16. In September 1994, Shake dedicated to Christiane a collection of 12 love poems with the title "Palm and Octopus". They were incorporated as Book 4 in his *Collected Poems*.
17. Christiane Keane, letter to Mitchell, 1999.
18. Ramanan, email correspondence, 2020.
19. Julian Keane, a BBC World Service journalist, died in 2019.
20. Ramanan, email correspondence, 2020.
21. The 14th CARIFESTA was held in Trinidad and Tobago in 2019.
22. Keane, *Collected Poems*, 48-49.
23. Kenneth John, "Shake Keane: The Final Rites," *The Vincentian*, November 19, 1999, 6.
24. Shake Keane, interview with Peter Clayton, *Sounds of Jazz*, BBC, 1998.
25. James Mitchell, *Beyond the Islands* (London: Macmillan Caribbean, 2006), 150.

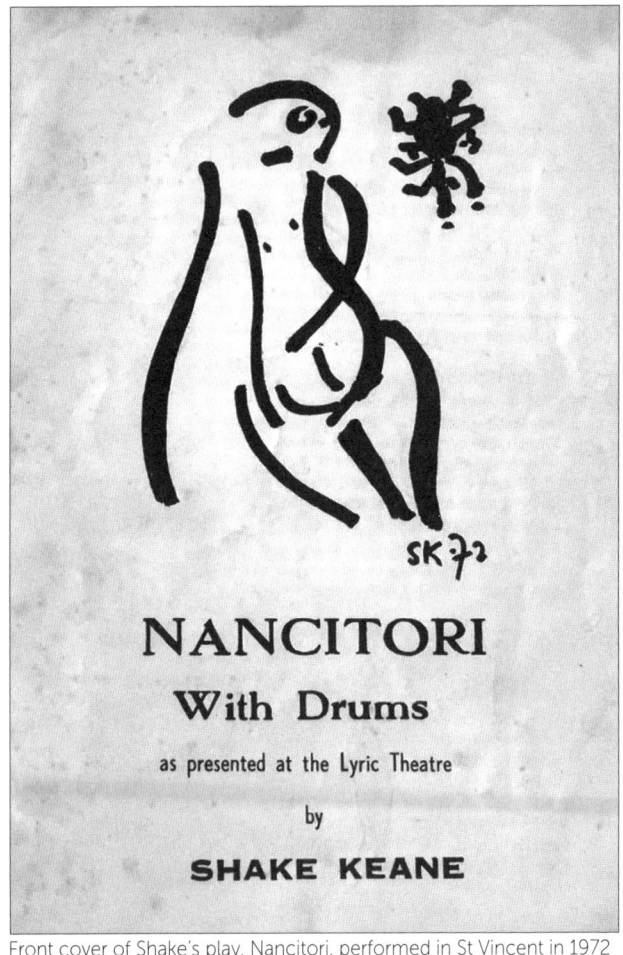

Front cover of Shake's play, Nancitori, performed in St Vincent in 1972 while he was still Director of Culture.

5 / 'THERE'S NO UP WITHOUT A DOWN'

And I
Lighter than the earth
heavier than mud
Have flown too far north

Far too far north
From home[1]

Shake returned to an island whose political landscape had changed dramatically. In taking up a senior post in government after an absence of more than two decades, it is possible that he was not fully aware of the instability of the political milieu. It seems that this decision came from his wish to make a cultural contribution to St Vincent's development reinforced by his headstrong nature once he had decided to return. Roland Ramanan reflected that a number of voices counselled against the decision to return, not least Elizabeth: 'My mother knew that returning to St Vincent was a mistake and so did many others.'[2] Christiane reflected on Shake's stubbornness in a letter to Mitchell after Shake died: 'When Shake had his mind on something, he would never change it.'[3] In the event and with the benefit of hindsight and to his own detriment, he greatly underestimated St Vincent's political environment.

By 1961 St Vincent politics had become a two-party race for political power. Party loyalty among the rank and file membership of the People's Political Party (PPP), formed in 1952 — the year that Shake left St Vincent — and led by Ebenezer Joshua, an ex-teacher and trade unionist, and its political opponent, the St Vincent Labour Party (SVLP), formed in 1955 and led by Milton Cato, a World War Two veteran and lawyer, was fiercely tribal. This sense of loyalty, however, did not extend to the politicians of either party who, with little thought of ideological commitment, regularly crossed the floor of the island's parliament if personal advantage might follow.

The period from 1972-1974 had been particularly turbulent. During these three years, the island's acting Attorney General had been murdered, and civil society groups, like the Educational Forum of the People and other community-based activist organisations, were arguing for independence. In 1972, the year before Shake returned to St Vincent, the balance of political power was precarious. Before the election of that year, James 'Son' Mitchell had won his seat in the parliament as an independent. With an equal number of seats between the PPP and the SVLP, he held the balance of political power, and negotiated successfully to become the island's Premier, with Joshua (the PPP leader) as his deputy. But this would be a short-lived arrangement. It was in these fraught political times that Shake returned home to take up his post as Director of the newly established Department of Culture.

In 1973, eight weeks after taking up his post, Shake presented a wide-ranging address to a national youth council convention. He expressed his commitment to the task of developing the country's artistic culture and laid out ambitious plans for his department's cultural activities. He began the talk simply, by saying: 'My name is Shake Keane and I have just come home from 21 years abroad.' He described the job as one 'for which my whole life seems to have been one long, steady preparation.' He argued that what was needed for cultural development was 'judgment and discretion without which all thinking and art is nothing but an explosion of concern, a riot of faith.'[4] He prioritised the importance of training in a variety of arts including school and community choirs, particularly at the primary level, pan tuning, dance, fine art and stage management, as well as the formation of school bands and a variety of festivals. Among the tasks he laid out for his department were obtaining sponsorship, contacting and working with similar departments in other islands, assisting individual artists and community groups and sponsoring and encouraging the development of local literature. These views were incorporated in a report on his department's 1974 activities. It was the first ever attempt to establish a programme of cultural development for St Vincent and the Grenadines.[5]

The implementation of these aims, however, was quickly scuppered by political changes that had extreme repercussions for Shake personally. By 1974 Joshua, Mitchell's deputy, and his wife Ivy, who also held a seat in government, found the power-sharing arrangement intolerable and both resigned from Mitchell's administration. which duly fell following the general election of 1974, in which the SVLP, led by Milton Cato, took ten of the 13 seats. The incoming government was unsympathetic to both Shake and the cultural department. In 1975 he was sacked and his post — and his department — disbanded. Mitchell wrote in his autobiography, *Beyond the Islands*, that Shake's sacking was an inevitable political response to any institutions that he, Mitchell, had created.[6]

Blazer Williams, a cultural commentator at the time, thought that the appointment of Shake, an 'outsider' on a relatively high salary who was not from within the Civil Service, had ruffled feathers among professional civil servants. As he bluntly claimed: 'Many civil servants were jealous because somebody who did not move up the ranks in the service was appointed director. The Civil Service Association… disliked the idea of the director earning a higher salary than the headmaster and headmistress of the Boys' Grammar School and the Girls' High School respectively."[7] The attempt to develop a department of culture in the public service was given a narrow and uncompromising epitaph by an incoming minister of government, who claimed dryly, 'You can't eat culture.' It took many years for a post of cultural officer to be reinstated.

Small island politics is also invariably personal. And so it was for Shake and Mitchell. Their continuing association was no secret. Mitchell lodged at Shake's comfortable home in the southern Cane Hall hills of St Vincent. Shake's then wife, Lou, would later be employed as assistant manager of Mitchell's hotel, the Frangipani, in Bequia. In turn, Shake's loyalty to Mitchell was illustrated in 1976 when he played as featured artist at the launch of Mitchell's New Democratic Party (NDP). 'My main everlasting memory of Shake was when I was living with him and wife Lou, and he drove with me to hold the first convention of the New Democratic Party which I was in the process of founding on the steps of a rum shop. The year was late 1976. Shake played a piece on his personal flugelhorn that had been made for him in Germany. The melody reverberated in the hills around. When he was finished, an old lady came up to us and said, "When I get to Heaven I want to hear music like that".[8] In 1999 Kenneth John offered a journalist's pithy summary of the events in his column for *The Vincentian*. John wrote: 'His [SK's] offence grew out of his friendship with "Son" Mitchell and the fact that he could not resist the temptation of sounding his flugelhorn at the NDP convention in Greggs.'[9]

Edgar Adams, an ophthalmologist, was the owner of the Fishnet Bar and Restaurant in the heart of Kingstown at the time. Shake and his friends including 'Blazer' Williams, the historian Adrian Fraser and others often gathered there. According to Adams, then a close confidant, Shake was in shock at his dismissal from his post and was, for a while, at a loss as to what action to take. In the event he was rescued to teach at Bishop's College, Georgetown, where he had to spend the week, coming back home for weekends. Lou had been teaching at the Girls' High School, but it was at this point, with Shake drinking heavily, that their marriage fell apart. Mitchell, who was perhaps closest to Shake at this time, observed: 'He was devastated by the loss of his job, but did not break down. He took it in his stride.[10]

Shake then moved schools to teach at the Intermediate High School, a small private school in Kingstown. Teaching in this school was a demanding job. The school comprised a long, barn-like, single storey structure at the eastern end of the town. Today the building stands padlocked, an abandoned and decaying shell, its red galvanised roof turning to rust. In 1979 it was a busy place with some 80 secondary level pupils. At the front was the principal's office, behind which was a single large room housing all six or so of the school's classes, divided only by a freestanding blackboard, in a feeble attempt to differentiate one class from the next. During lessons, each teacher struggled to be heard as the class behind the nearest blackboard might suddenly begin, in unison, to recite their times tables. In 1979, it was in such a daily cacophony that Shake was working.

However, teaching did help him recover from what he hints was a bout of depression. After John LaRose, co-owner (with his wife Sarah White) of the London-based New Beacon Books, the publishing house and bookshop, visited him in St Vincent in 1978, he apologised in a letter for a two-year silence, explaining that he, 'simply went into isolation for a long while, finding all kinds of unexpected sores to lick.' Teaching helped him to survive by showing him that, 'Talking to people every day is turning out to be quite useful and settling.'[11]

Despite such difficulties his poetry flourished. In 1979, his collection *One A Week With Water: Rhymes and Notes* was awarded Cuban's prestigious Casa de las Américas regional prize for poetry from the English-speaking Caribbean. That the collection was submitted at all was fortuitous. As told by his friend Son Mitchell: 'On one occasion while with him at home in Cane Hall I saw the ad for the Caribbean poetry competition in Cuba. I collected his poems scattered in the house, had him sign the competition form and posted them to Cuba.' Apparently, when Shake heard that he had won the prize, he phoned Mitchell with the words, '*We* won.'[12] In his circumstances, this was no small achicvement caught as he was between the demands of school teaching and returning to playing music as a humble, jobbing musician.

Even so, Shake was now in the unenviable position of being an internationally acclaimed jazz musician whose change of career had been undone by politics and had gone disastrously wrong. Musically, too, he must have felt dismayed. There were no musicians of his stature with whom to play or to stretch his talent.

For a few years in the 1970s, Shake played at the Aquatic Club, overlooking Villa Beach on the south coast of St Vincent. A wide veranda overlooks the beach and protruding jetty. It was for years the place where the island's white colonial elite came to play — swim, moor their boats, drink, dance, and gossip. In the 1970s, the Club was bought, without a name change, by Stilton (known to all locally as 'Stilly') Fraser, a returned black middle-class Vincentian who had made his money in Toronto. As he liked to remind me, in the past neither he nor Shake would have been allowed in — unless they were there to serve drinks or play music. Stilly threw its doors open to anyone. On weekends he regularly hosted touring calypsonians and other popular visiting bands. So for an hour or two every Wednesday evening, Shake played standard tunes with an accompanying pianist for the weekly 'sing-along'.

Shake hated the experience, but funds were tight and this provided a regular supplement to school teaching. After performing his set he would sit at the bar with brandy glass and roll-up cigarette, complaining, to whoever would listen, about the low level of music he was required to accompany.

One weekend in 1979, a touring band from Trinidad came through and played two gigs. The Saturday night gig, which was widely promoted, featured Shake as guest performer. The band leader was Gene Lawrence, the Vincentian-born, classically trained guitarist, with a wide range of music at his command. He invited Shake to play with his small combo of electric guitar and piano, bass and drummer. The evening was sold out. Stilly admitted that since he had taken over the Club he had never seen so diverse a crowd at the venue. One tune Shake nominated was 'Moonlight in Vermont'. Once the band found the correct key, Shake, standing to the side of the bandstand, flexed his fingers a few times, put the flugelhorn to his lips and played the tender ballad in a precise, lyrical manner. The poignant sound of his horn rose to the roof and seeped out into the cool night air. The dancing stopped. Conversation ceased. In awe, punters slowly shook their heads.

Musically, the evening was a rare lift, but even this band was playing what people wanted to hear. This was a low period of Shake's musical career — his contacts in the jazz world in Britain and Europe had receded, and he could see only a bleak future if he remained on the island. As a schoolboy, he and his friend Cecil Cyrus often debated

Poster for CARIFESTA, the fourth Caribbean regional arts festival, held in 1981 in Barbados. (*Courtesy National Cultural Foundation, Bridgetown, Barbados*)

the maxim: 'There's no up without a down.' Its pessimism and fatalism seemed to foreshadow both his current situation and later experience, but this was far from the full picture. Before leaving St Vincent for the first time he had drawn a more subtle picture of life's experiences in 'Barrouallie Dawn', a poem he wrote in 1947, that extended the simplistic up or down metaphor: 'The best staircases are spiral. For to venture/Upward or downward is to venture in many directions.'[13]

Just before Shake left St Vincent for the second time, this time for New York City, one of his last acts was to contribute as a soloist in CARIFESTA IV, in 1981, in Barbados. Together with British/Jamaican poet musician Linton Kwesi Johnson, the British TV documentarist Anthony Wall was in Barbados to direct a film portrait of the festival. At the last minute Wall negotiated with Shake to contribute to the film. Shake's involvement cemented a long-standing friendship with

Johnson who wrote and produced the film. It captures Shake performing his poem *The Volcano Suite* and later, standing on a Barbados beach, his trousers half rolled up, he plays a soulful flugelhorn to the sea.[14] Looked at now, it seems to express a sense of the ending of his heartfelt affair with St Vincent. There was a mixture of sadness and some bitterness. In the interview with Peter Clayton in 1988 he observed flatly: 'The teaching and playing was getting nowhere so New York was the easiest place to go to and the most affordable.' When asked, 'How did New York turn out for you?' He tellingly stated: 'I wanted to get out of St Vincent not that I wanted to go to the States.'[15]

An exasperated love affair with his island and its people was over. And so, in 1981, frustrated and somewhat embittered, he left St Vincent for the last time and would never return.

Notes

1 Shake Keane, "On a Plane," unpublished poem, 1992. See Appendix 1 for the full text.
2 Ramanan, email correspondence, 2020.
3 Christiane Keane, letter to Mitchell.
4 Ellsworth McG Keane (Shake Keane), "Feature Address," Convention of the National Youth Council, Georgetown, St Vincent, July 27, 1973.
5 Department of Culture: Projects, Priorities, Plans 1974/1975, Director of Culture, Kingstown May 23, 1975.
6 Mitchell, *Beyond the Islands*, 150.
7 Blazer Williams, "Some Thoughts on the Abolition of the Department of Culture: Courting the Culture of Death," *Nam Speaks*, 1, no.2, 1975, 8-14.
8 Mitchell, interview.
9 Kenneth John, "Shake Keane: The Final Rites," *The Vincentian*, November 19, 1999, 6.
10 Mitchell, interview.
11 Shake Keane, letter to John LaRose, June 27, 1980, George Padmore Institute Archive, London.
12 Mitchell, interview.
13 Keane, *Collected Poems*, 58.
14 *Brixton to Barbados*, BBC Two, Arena, 1981.
15 Clayton, interview.

The Volcano Suite was Shake's poetic response to St Vincent's volcano which erupted in 1979. (*Cover by Owen 'Sap' Coombs*)

6/THE 'LADEN GARDEN' OF POETRY

Writing about an artist with two developed talents, music and poetry, is different from writing about those who have a particular trajectory that can be teased out and followed. Clearly this isn't Shake's trajectory, so writing about his poetry means trying to understand from his writing what's happening in his head. The story to be told is not so much that this happened, then this and then he expressed it like this. He does respond to externals, of course — the St Vincent environment, the volcanic eruption that he witnessed in 1979, his situation in New York. And his behaviour with women — the serial dependent marriages — was not unusual for Caribbean men and musicians. But it's worth stressing that his reactions to events and situations are those of a jazz artist. In other words, one who is located at the crossroads between two disciplines, who understands their rules but chooses to break them or interpret them in his own way and take the chance that he will be understood. As we will see, particularly in his mature work, he often applies what could be called a jazz rule-breaking style to the composition of poetry. This ranges from a particular way of 'playing' with a subject to how a poem is orchestrated visually on the page.

Shake's literary sensibilities were shaped by religious belief, the modern classics, the Vincentian 'islandness' of his West Indian identity and the world of school teaching. More important, however, was the way he used these influences in his writing, putting his learning to use while interrogating received priorities and privileging a local voice.

Though for the most part he wrote regularly, there was a 10-year gap from 1957 to 1966 when he was in London. Inspiration to write poetry appears to have deserted him during these years though he was confident that it would return; which it did to a limited extent, first in Germany and more forcefully when he returned to St Vincent and later in New York. In total, Shake's output was relatively small. *The Angel Horn: Collected Poems*, published posthumously in 2005, has 72 poems and 182 pages. His most prestigious collection, *One A Week With Water: Rhymes and Notes (OWWW)*, runs to 74 pages. Though this collection had won the Casa de las Américas prize for Anglophone poetry, only 500 copies were printed and it has never been republished. The two early collections, *L'Oubli* (1950) and *Ixion* (1952), published in his twenties, and *The Volcano Suite*, a long poem published in 1979, all slim, self-published works, are even more difficult to find. By any conventional measure (volume of output, impact and status) therefore, Shake would be considered a 'minor' poet. In addition, perhaps due to the limited exposure that his writing enjoyed, in his later years he also described himself as 'a good poet of the second rank'.[1]

He is 'minor' in another way as well: as champion of the unofficial and informal Caribbean world. His St Vincent poems dwell on the local, sometimes with affection, at others with humour and irony. We are accustomed to this from novelists like Sam Selvon, VS Naipaul and Anthony Winkler, but undercutting poetry's high seriousness is perhaps more risky if a poet is to be noticed and acclaimed. And in Shake's case, the addition of an improvisational, apparently casual style, involving jazz — riffs, playing with time, fragmented lines and typographical experimentation — all part of *OWWW* — make much of his work unconventional and resistant to easy categorisation.

In England, Shake would continue to articulate this sense of commitment to the local. Interviewed by the editor of the anthology, Rosalie Murphy, in 1970 about his contribution to *Contemporary Poets of the English Language*, he described his writing as reflecting: 'Typical West Indian consciousness {with themes of} self-realisation through nature, nationalism, sense of the unreality of colonial life; therefore, social protest on one hand, and on another {an} obsession with identity after death since present life seems unreal. On the positive side an attempt to understand and restructure poetically the tragedy, hope, conservatism and ecstasy of peasant and folk life.'[2]

Over a span of 50 years, Shake's writing exhibits a range of themes that dramatise these characteristics: poems of more formal faith as well as the spiritual life-force of nature, poems of place exploring 'the local' through landscape, language and individuals, poems of social commentary that employ satire and mockery and, finally, sometimes melancholic poems about love and art (see Chapter 8). Shake's term for the specific tone or voice of each poem was 'atmosphere', and its foremost quality was optimism.

As early as 1950, in 'Some Religious Attitudes in West Indian Poetry', published in *Bim*, he argued that the purpose of poetry is to produce delight. He meant this in both a spiritual sense and in the sense of entertainment. Late in life he returned to this theme in an interview, when, talking about the satisfaction of making poetry, he argued that poetry is both communication (subject matter) and expression (technique), and that both offer elements of delight. He explained that for himself, as a practising poet: 'Joy in poetry comes out of solving a problem — a verbal conundrum — a matter of trying to solve the problems of words, their weight and tone — when you think you've solved it you get joy out of that.'[3]

Beyond his childhood efforts to entertain his family with dialect verse, the poetry written when he was a young man in St Vincent offers a way into understanding his philosophy and changing outlook on life. The early writing was informed by a combination of Shake's colonial education and his family's strong religious leaning. As a young man he took his faith seriously, applying both a personal and an analytical approach to belief. What he called 'joy' and 'delight' manifested in an underlying optimism which endured throughout his life, despite bouts of depression, dependence on alcohol and frustration with his under-appreciated musical career. Literary influences on his early poetry include the Bible and the classics. In a letter to Cecil Cyrus, he discussed both these influences in a poem, 'Recitative for Christmas', that he had submitted in 1950 to *Caribbean Voices*:

I was born there, yesterday,
Long ago, under doom
Of a thousand prophesies,...

For I am also He
Who flamed in the bush for a token
And in the sky for a covenant
And in two walled sins
Down in the plain of the pillar of salt...
There in the heart of that clay
I have always been born.[4]

He explains the poem in the following way: 'It is written in the Biblical style, and in it you will see that my faith is beginning to congeal into something capable of expression in consistent terms. I have made free use of certain Bible stories, like the destruction of Sodom and the Pillars of Salt etc. and I have tried to link the Philosophy that was born at Bethlehem with certain actual conditions in the West Indies which seem to be a definite denial of that philosophy.'[5] He simultaneously critiques the style of the poem while revealing, with a younger man's assurance, it as a landmark: 'The similes, I'm afraid, are a bit Virgilian; but on the whole the poem now strikes me as a sign of approaching maturity.'[6]

In his writings for *Bim* on religious attitudes in West Indian poetry, he discussed, in two separate articles, both Biblical and classical influences among Caribbean poets of the period. His concern was to tease out how West Indian poetry of the 1940s and 1950s was informed by nature and religion, arguing that the landscape is central to this relationship. He found common ground with AJ Seymour, the Guyanese poet and editor of *Kyk-Over-Al,* in the perception that the English-speaking tradition of Caribbean poetry afforded an expression of deferred and hidden aspects of ancient religious impulses from Egypt and sub-Saharan Africa. He also argued that this mode of belief was not a form of animism. Rather, nature is understood as a path to the apprehension of God, involving a contemplation of beauty, mystery, terror and other encompassing emotions, and through them a Being who must have been their creator.[7] Nature, then, is apprehended as a teacher or symbol of a deeper truth — a 'Natural Presence', as he put it later — with which humanity has to come to terms. We are more relaxed about such ideas in the twenty-first century, but the expression of a similar notion in the poetry of a young Derek Walcott, Shake's contemporary, led him into conflict with the Catholic authorities in St Lucia around this time.

Like Walcott, Shake was open to a wide range of literary influences, both classical and modern. A hint of the classics is there in the title of his second collection, *Ixion*,[8] published in 1952. The four poems in this collection ('Storm Season', 'Four Secrets', 'Poem for R…' and 'Mirrors') play with the idea of perpetual motion, flux or what Ezra Pound called 'unstill'. The challenges they throw up are resolved in a somewhat forced optimism, which concludes the fourth poem in the collection, when he writes:

> *But in the breaking surf and the brain*
> *I see children, little futures loud in the*
> *braying spray,*
> *Brown shining limbs shattering the*
> *blue mirror,*
> *Shooting up alive from the breathtaking*
> * death*
> *Of the dived sea,*
> *Laughing in the red-faced dusk,*
> *   laughing.*[9]

This collection and *L'Oubli: Poems* contain meditative poems in a modernist style reflecting a young poet's conflicting moods alongside a sense of Caribbean spirituality. He acknowledged the closeness of influence when he described his early writing as a West Indian version of modern English poetry of the 1930s. Eliot's *The Waste Land*, in particular, appears to have been a major influence on 'L'Oubli', the long poem that leads the first collection, which explores the paradox that to live is to forget and to remember is to die. It offers a meditation on death and the transience of life, couched in terms of the soul's simultaneous longing for and refusal of God. Here the joy or delight that he values in poetry comes from his technique in creating a finely worked poem that plays with paradox, repetition of key words and the shifting personae that include 'you', the author, and the 'voice from heaven' that states:

Seek me, O restless soul,
No rest for the seeking soul.[10]

Two of the poems in the collection attracted the attention of such Caribbean literary critics as Gordon Rohlehr and Edward Baugh. Rohlehr saw in 'Shaker Funeral' an imaginative fusion of religious feeling with the energy of oral tradition.[11] In the same collection, Baugh drew attention to his use of early jazz inflections in the poem 'Calypso Dancer', a feature for which other poets, notably Kamau Brathwaite, would later become known.[12] Lloyd Brown, the Jamaican literary critic and author of the pioneering work of criticism, *West Indian Poetry*, also gave Shake's early poetry critical attention, noting common ground with that of the Tobagonian poet Eric Roach, in particular. Brown read Shake's early poetry as going beyond Roach's work, while offering a sense of renewal and 'new beginnings out of fragments of the past'.[13]

The themes of exploration and celebration of new beginnings, which characterise Shake's *Collected Poems*, reach their height in *One A Week With Water*. Many of the poems that he wrote after this collection, especially those written in New York, focus on more intimate locations of city life — for example the pub and bar where he often sat to write — as he moved away from wider philosophical concerns or cityscapes. In times of success as well as bleaker moments of upheaval and despair, Shake returned time and again to writing poetry. Whatever his circumstances, most of his poems retain his humour and a willingness to entertain, whether his intended readers were children or adults.

Another of his themes is the exploration of nature in a Caribbean context. He often demonstrates how people are a part of the island landscape. The early poem, 'Barrouallie Dawn', observes: 'Already children are returning/over the mud sided valley over Glebe Hill with their bundles of bush' and how 'Mango season/fruit fights delight in doorways of mud and wattle.'[14] When he came to write *The Volcano Suite* in 1979, inspired by the eruption of La Soufrière, St Vincent's volcano, a devastated landscape is once again infused with his trademark optimism.[15]

Yet another influence on Shake's writing — both in terms of how he wrote and who he wrote for — was his ongoing interest in education in general and teaching in particular. His involvement with the profession lent him a quality that could be described as 'teacherliness' — leading the reader with a lightness of touch, authoritatively but without bombast. Signs of a teacher's playfulness can be seen in the numerous references to teaching and young people throughout his writing, as in Book 3 of *Collected Poems*, subtitled 'Thirteen Studies in Home Economics', where each study is referred to as a 'lesson'. In *Collected Poems*, Book 1, the playful child centredness of titles like 'Hide and Seek', 'Girls and Boys' and 'Unu Coonoomoonoo' show him reaching out to young readers. One example — recollected by Son Mitchell as having been written in one sitting in London, on 26 December 1972 — for the son of a friend, six-year-old Dan Beglan, is reproduced as WEEK FIFTY-ONE in *OWWW*:

once the wind
said to the sea
I am sad

THE 'LADEN GARDEN' OF POETRY

>   *And the sea said*
> *Why*
>   *And the wind said*
> *Because I*
> *am not blue like the sky*
> *or like you*
>
>   *So the sea said what's*
> *so sad about that*
>
>   *Lots*
> *of things are blue*
> *or red or other colors too*
>   *But nothing*
> *neither sea nor sky*
> *can blow so strong*
> *or sing so long as you*
>
>   *And the sea looked sad*
>   *So the wind said*
> *Why*[16]

In *OWWW* he also provides pithy notes on the process of growing up, and his commitment to education is directly expressed in the dedication at the start of *OWWW*, dated 11 March 1976: 'For the girls and boys of Bishop's College, Georgetown, St Vincent, who tried hard to accept me as their Principal.'[17]

To illustrate the presence of this underlying optimism in much of his writing and even in trying circumstances, I will jump ahead to 1979. In mid-April that year came the violent eruption of La Soufrière. It has been active throughout the island's history, with known periodic explosive eruptions, many of which involved lava flows and *nuée ardentes*, glowing clouds of volcanic ash. The population of the northern half of the island was forced to evacuate to the southern half for some 11 weeks, leading to widespread social disruption as schools and other public buildings in the southern part of the island became shelters for villagers. The instability of Shake's personal circumstances compounded by the eruption could have made him reconsider his earlier more optimistic world view. It would not have been surprising if he had seen the volcanic eruption exclusively in terms of dread and destruction, but when he came to write about it, his thinking was more profound, universal and optimistic.

Within three weeks of the eruption, Shake had written and self-published a collection of five poems on the eruption and its consequences, which he called *The Volcano Suite*. Introducing them, he describes them as 'contemplations' and draws attention to the 'original and permanent' forces released by the eruptions: 'They form a Natural Presence (sic), which is coordinated with our presence on this planet. And nothing is more basic to our existence as humans than this understanding of our relationship with this Presence.'[18]

More than simply recognising disaster and a changed landscape, the volcano poems embrace the idea of the renewal of community out of disruption and chaos. He interprets this collective experience as 'a vision of a future composed not merely of the will to survive, but the practical necessity of love for one another, within the coordinates of that Presence'. In the fifth poem of *The Volcano Suite* he expresses this thought in the following way:

> *1979 was the year the people*
> *started to begin to learn*
> *to understand that they must begin to learn*
> *to love one another.*[19]

THE 'LADEN GARDEN' OF POETRY

Each poem explores a different development or opportunity afforded by the eruptions. And so in the first poem he observes that the island 'fell in love with itself', and notes in parenthesis: 'As a prelude to resurrection and brotherly love/you can't beat ructions and eruptions.'[20] In the second poem he identifies one of the new things that is born as the learning of words associated with volcanic eruption: 'It will be impossible to recollect my life/without the knowledge of certain words — Magma, ejectamenta, Larikai.'[21] The third and fourth poems identify language respectively as a form of resistance to volcanic chaos and what the islanders have in common: 'how similar our private lives are.' And he goes on to make a vow:

next christmas
i
shall buy
my linoleum
in broad daylight
so strangers
can laugh
beforehand
at my preferences
and love me
on that morning[22]

Finally, the fifth poem offers hope for the future by focusing attention on a couple who,

...were in love
and their garden was laden.[23]

His writing leaves a legacy of direct interest to the Caribbean, especially his native St Vincent as early religious and contemplative themes gave way to an interest in the secular oral tradition. As we will see in the next chapter, his underlying jazz influences are increasingly apparent in the way he uses each page of poetry, splaying words around like single notes, sometimes with serious intent and sometimes humorously. They are forms of 'nonsense' that he claimed as his own. Here his power over the word and his word play come together to provide a commentary on Caribbean folk culture, the nature of order and its obverse, chaos — often in the context of a commentary on Vincentian society. His deft and original use of linguistic improvisation startles us into laughter or unsettles our expectations.

Notes

1 Austin, interview.
2 Ellsworth McGranahan Keane. In *Contemporary Poets of the English Language*, ed. Rosalie Murphy (London: St Martin's Press, 1970), 187.
3 Austin, interview.
4 Shake Keane, letter to Cecil Cyrus, November 25, 1950. For the full text of the poem see Appendix 2.
5 Letter to Cyrus.
6 Letter to Cyrus.
7 Ellsworth McG. Keane, "Some Religious Attitudes in West Indian Poetry," *Bim* 4, No 16, (1952), 267.
8 Ixion is a minor character in Homer's *Iliad*. A king from Thessaly who was punished by Zeus for attempting to seduce his wife, Hera, he was bound to an eternally revolving wheel in Tartarus.
9 Ellsworth McGranahan Keane, *Ixion*, self-published (1952), 14.
10 Ellsworth McGranahan Keane, *L'Oubli. Poems*, self-published (1950), 7.
11 Gordon Rohlehr, "The Problem of the Problem of Form" in *The Shape of that Hurt and Other Essays* (Trinidad: Longman Ltd, 1992), 21.
12 Edward Baugh, "West Indian Poetry, 1900-1970, A Study in Cultural Decolonisation," pamphlet no1 (Kingston, Jamaica: Savacou Publications, 1971), 3.
13 Lloyd Brown, *West Indian Poetry* (Boston: Twayne, 1978), 73.
14 Keane, *Collected Poems*, 55, 56.
15 *Brixton to Barbados*, 1981. See https://www.youtube.com/watch?v=txYYtHHnKcQ for Shake Keane's filmed reading of *The Volcano Suite*.
16 Keane, *OWWW*, 68. Chosen as "Poem of the day", 2011, http://www.littleblogofstories.com/2011/04/poem-of-day-april-4.html.

17 Keane, *OWWW*, 9.
18 Ellsworth McG. Keane, *The Volcano Suite: A Series of Five Poems*, self-published (1979), 1.
19 Keane, *The Volcano Suite*, 20.
20 Keane, *The Volcano Suite*, 2.
21 Keane, *The Volcano Suite*, 9.
22 Keane, *The Volcano Suite*, 13.
23 Keane, *The Volcano Suite*, 19.

Cover of *The Angel Horn: Shake Keane Collected Poems (1927-1997)*.
(*Courtesy House of Nehesi Publishers*)

7 / CROSSROADS OF JAZZ AND POETRY

Shake's poetry was strongly influenced by his development as a jazz musician. He spoke about this cross-influencing on a return visit to London in 1992. Discussing jazz and poetry with Michael Garrick and Linton Kwesi Johnson for BBC TV, he captured the influence of jazz on other genres and styles, including poetry, in the following way: 'There are certain kinds of structure, certain habits, that all jazz men seem to have, and if you find a poem that uses what would parallel those habits you might say, for example, "that is a jazz poem." For example the riff, the repeated phrase, that happens in jazz a lot. Then you have the sudden juxtaposition of certain elements. Then there is the feeling that the poem is improvised but some [poems] are highly crafted but don't strike you as highly crafted. If you pick out these elements and find them in other writing or way of dress or ways of talking you can say that is a jazz man, or that is a jazz hat, jazz poem or jazz novel.'[1]

The tone and structure of this informal statement are subject to the continuing influence of 'teacherliness'. It's there in the way he defines the term 'riff', and the many examples he gives to illustrate 'jazz' ways of doing things. How might jazz notions of riffing, juxtaposition, improvisation and apparent spontaneity be seen in his writing?

A poem that carries some of these influences is 'Lesson Seven' of *Collected Poems*. Also called 'Credential',[2] he performed it with backing music on the 1991 CD *Real Keen: Reggae into Jazz*, his last studio venture. Improvising on the notion of 'play' and 'playing', it also juxtaposes the lighter and darker shades of Shake's life as poet and musician. As Val Wilmer writes on the sleeve notes, this is 'an autobiographical tale of a boy raised by a music-loving father who taught him to honour his horn and himself, and who fails to encounter appreciation for these priorities either in Europe or back home.'

The dilemma of the returned migrant is starkly captured in these three lines:

All-we culture all-we potential
is definightly non-residential.
all dis trumpet is a famous load o'piss.[3]

Wilmer also singled out the renegade element in Keane's lifestyle as much as his artistry. In response to the rejection, 'his solution is to go his own way and follow a bohemian existence. He exposes his disdain for middle-class values in a manner as pithy as the way he attacks a tune with his horn.'[4] This feature of his headstrong nature — evinced in his determination to return to St Vincent, and to keep touring despite later ill-health — was a central part of his lifestyle.

What are we to make of what Wilmer calls his 'disdain' in this poem? On the face of it, the poem appears to reflect little 'joy' and offer little 'delight'. On one level, Shake felt hard done by in his dealings with the institutions of government and society. The closure of the Department of Culture he had returned to lead, and the undervaluing of his musicianship at 'home', were difficult events and attitudes with which to come to terms. They resulted in the sense of incomprehension and exclusion that he expressed in a letter to John LaRose in London, after some seven years in St Vincent: 'St Vincent still baffles me. Life here seems to defy participation.'[5]

The experience of irrelevance and rejection poses the question, can one ever actually return? In the interval between departure and return, both place and person change. So where might 'delight' be located? Delight can be taken from the technical accomplishment of the poem, as a well-structured tale that takes the reader from childhood to maturity with no little humour, and reaches a climax with his decision that he will simply have to go his own way and please himself. The poem ends in the following way:

> *So Ah hice up me credential*
> *same one wha' me farder show*
> *how fe polish*
> *how fe respec'*
> *how fe blow*
> *An'Ah say...// 3/4!Sxhf=+f@@@....*[6]

As subject matter, beyond articulating his feeling of rejection of his role and skills, beyond his ranting and dissatisfaction, 'Credential' poignantly expresses the idea that homecoming will often be accompanied by disappointment. In recognising that ultimately the migrant can never really return, 'Credential' is a valediction — a farewell to innocence.

If the tone of 'Credential' is valedictory, the long poem 'Roundtrip', which opens his *Collected Poems*, takes a more playful approach to migration and return. Starting with a small group of Vincentians in London, it soon spreads outwards to include all sorts of difference —

learning Norwegian, a Carib discovering his Amerindian background, Chinese, Spanish, Africans…Then the Vincentians become West Indians, the one learning Norwegian *becomes* 'the Norwegian', 'a Spanish chap' turns out to come from Panama, a Chinese turns out to be Jamaican, someone called Creighton comes from Pakistan… all of this happens in London, a place where everything can become something else and words can mean different things at the same time. By playing with language, altering famous names as in 'James **Ballwin**', 'Mau tse Che', and 'Julius Nyereretung'[7] or creating malapropisms as in 'archangelist' for archaeologist, he suggests that shapeshifting is the nature of migration. After the shift from islander to West Indian, the next shift is to recognising blackness as the key to diasporic identity. So, 'We might still be calling ourselves that'[8] — that is, West Indian — if not for a dream where all the different black people get mixed up and start calling themselves sisters and brothers. The poem therefore dramatises a story of politicisation and self-definition, bringing about an expanding view of identity and belonging.

The poem goes on to show that when they get back home and try to reproduce what they had in London, it doesn't quite work: 'we not settling een **so** well'.[9] This is not only because the beer is not as good, but because they have come back with an expanded consciousness which can not now be accommodated in a single place, or small island, or singular point of view. The pull towards home is counterpoised by the scattering to all points of the globe, as shown in snippets of news from ex-London friends around the world. Like it or not, the migrants are now part of a global community and can not easily reclaim their old Vincentian identity. As a result, one of them has changed his name to Doku and buys himself *Teach Yourself Spanish*.[10]

The story, then, is one of an expanding consciousness, an education in different kinds of community and relationships, brought about by migration. Both gain and loss are involved, but the change is ineluctable and permanent. The linguistic vivacity and playfulness, however, ultimately privilege a sense of celebration over mourning. What is gained is more than what is lost. Linguistic playfulness, with rhymes and half rhymes dotted about, and the theme of play run throughout Shake's work, marking a fundamental association between his life as poet and as musician. For most people leisure is distinct from work. Professional musicians are perhaps one of the few groups of people in the modern world for whom this is not the case: for them, playing is their work and work their play. In Shake's writing, play is the freedom to invent, distort, change, say one thing and mean something else, or create an effect by the arrangement of words on a page. This finds its fullest expression in *OWWW*.

In terms of riffing or its near literary equivalent, genre bending, *OWWW* is a good example. The collection is essentially a one-year diary of weekly entries in which are kept personal notes recording strange or noteworthy words, folk sayings, reminiscences, lunar observations. The title, 'One A Week With Water,' sounds like a prescription, implying that he is offering regular relief for an unspoken or undiagnosed condition. Another theme is his play with calendar time and dates. Some weeks begin with a qualification — 'Yet even metals can show fatigue'[11] — as if an argument were being continued. Some weeks are consecutively out of order — *FORTY-THREE AND FORTY-TWO WEEKS* follow WEEK FORTY-FOUR. WEEK FORTY-SEVEN appears after WEEK FIFTY-THREE.

The collection is as much prose monologue, spoof bureaucratic form and letter writing as it is poetry as conventionally understood. There is, for example, his satirical spoof bureaucratic form that traces the history of a 'psychological patient'. Much of her career as set out on her form involves changing names to avoid vilification by rude nicknames given to her by her school classmates and compatriots. The fear begins at school when Shake records part of her early history:

> Mother's Name: Tricksy Norman
> (.....)
> name: priscilla isola
> HISTORY: Patient leaves Catholic Primary School after 2 weeks, dreading nicknames that could be built up from her initials e.g.: PIN; PNIS; or the grotesque PNIN. Problem persists regardless of use of mother's or father's family name.....
> Actual name used by schoolmates: PUNKNANCE MILLINGTON...[12]

Superficially this is knockabout stuff. A nickname in the Caribbean is a mark of familiarity which elevates the subject through friendship. But it is equally a form of abuse, usually derived from quirky aspects of the person named. Familiarity and bawdiness are simultaneously heightened by the play on Priscilla Isola's initials PNIS and PNIN. More can be read into this as Shake takes aim at the hallowed practice of *naming* in the Caribbean. The importance of naming has been a preoccupation of Derek Walcott (*Sea Grapes, Another Life* and *Tiepolo's Hound*) as much as Kamau Brathwaite (*X/Self*). In the 1970s it was fashionable to change one's name in order to register more closely an association with Africa. Indirectly, all this becomes Shake's target, which he both buries and revives with humour. Of course, should he want to be taken 'seriously', then this lightheartedness is perhaps not the best way to win the interest of 'serious' literary critics.

Another aspect of his work centred on the folk elements that inform Caribbean literature, in particular, his dramatisation of rural folk culture in the process of change. In *OWWW*, in particular, he used linguistic improvisation — which he calls 'nonsense' — to stretch the language, startle his readers into laughter and unsettle their expectations. For example, he draws attention to the liminal nature of words by raising the issue of how to name a village. As signifiers of oral culture, some words are not easily transcribed into writing. He notes in WEEK SIX:

BUM-BUM is a small but growing
village near the Capital of St. Vincent.
We have not yet devised a means
of spelling its name in a way
that satisfactorily indicates the way
it is pronounced.[13]

Here he challenges the non-Vincentian reader by not indicating how the highly suggestive name *should* be pronounced. At the same time, by drawing attention to the instability between spelling and pronunciation of the name of the village, he indicates the creative tension in naming and locating, a tension that involves the whole society.

Also in his footnotes to the main text — the subtitle of *OWWW* is 'Notes and Rhymes' — he orchestrates play with words in other ways. 'Truction', 'bodderation', 'long-guts', 'edge up', 'gutsify' and 'jokify'[14] are word creations that he offers the reader without comment as though challenging one to 'read' the experience through Vincentian

Cover of Shake's prize-winning poetry collection, 1979. (*Casa de las Américas*)

eyes. These neologisms or creolisations typify Vincentian speech patterns and suggest a creative, irreverent relationship with language. Here word power (power over the word) and word play come together in the creation of these new words, which are necessitated by local participation. Some of these words belong to unofficial culture, others he may have invented. It doesn't matter. As presented in his 'book', they become notes or atoms floating on the boundaries of official and unofficial worlds.

His improvisational technique, close to jazz riffs and refrains, can be found in the fragmented arrangements of the text and in the flouting of conventional expectations. The whole notion of poetry as a sinuous piece of writing utilising a particular form or pattern is discarded. Instead, the reader is required to participate, as in the oral tradition. In this context participation involves filling in the blanks in the text: this takes different forms. In a long monologue extending over a few weeks that he gives to an acquaintance, Faustina, whom he meets on the street, at times she is clearly answering questions that he has put that are not in the text. For example: ' … GLASSES?… No… I never had all those background with High School and soforth… Ohoo (?) oo!ooo?!… Is me sister, Avril, you taking me for all the time! *She* had glasses.'[15]

In other situations the reader is provided with a jigsaw of groups of words with which to make sense of the world that Shake has created. The jigsaw, in turn, allows a process of discovery. What the participation implies is that who constructs the world is important. Do we do it, or do we allow someone else to construct our world for us? Shake gives us the chance to make sense of it ourselves. An illustration of this is in WEEK THIRTY-THREE, from an apparently shouted conversation perhaps from one side of a street to another:

GYURL!

Brung-skin gyurl

    BRUNG-SKIN   *GYURL!!!*

What yo say?   *WHO?*

is only you-one, she sister, dey?
(thought you was in the USA)

listen Sis…

                You and WHO?

where de chile?

RIFF

> *the CHILE TOO?!*
>
> *o.k... You and You*
>
> *best hads miss me a while*[16]

But musicians, especially jazz musicians, and poets also play in other ways. They can take something familiar — a tune, tradition, story or nursery rhyme — and make it unfamiliar, reworking and changing it for different ends. We can see this in a number of poems in *Collected Poems: Angel Horn*. In one, he tells an animal folk tale about the fox and turtle in his own way. When fox races up a thorny gru-gru tree ahead of turtle and swallows the tender shoot at the top and is asked by turtle why he did that, he replies: 'It seemed a good idea at the time!'[17] A short poem, 'Family Figgers', plays with the traditional method that children are taught when doing simple arithmetical division.

> *2 into 1*
> *yo can't*
> *borry 0*
> *2 into 10 equals 5*
>
> *5 into 1 yo can't*
> *beg for 0*
> *yo can't but*
> *5 into 10 equals 2*
>
> *and 2 into 2 yo can*
> *So steal 1*
>
> *yo can't*[18]

The spontaneity of play gives rise to an element of disorderliness that operates on at least two levels. In 'Credential', Shake regularly repeats the elliptical statement: 'me farder didn' gie me dat but 'e gimme dis,'[4] in response to the different demands that his girlfriend, the 'Mudder Country' and Vincentian society in turn place on him. These demands might involve cash, material possessions or good breeding, or be in the form of a blunt rejection of his chosen art form. The refrain also hints at a link between his sexual credentials and his musical credentials, left unstated until his patience is exhausted and 'rudeness' enters the poem. Rude interventions upset decorum, create embarrassment and push encounters out of control. Rudeness is also a speech form associated with anger. Rather than promoting disorderliness for its own sake, it is a challenge to established forms of order. As such, 'Credential' marks an artistic turning point, offsetting anger and frustration with humour. Finding himself taunted each way he turns, Shake's blunt final expletive indicates that he sees no option but to go his own way and please himself. In this way he expresses his intention to remain true to his art — his trumpet playing and his poetry — whatever the cost.

Shake has remained a minor poet in the conventional sense that not many critics have examined his poetry. Perhaps for these reasons and with a few exceptions in his early writing, his writing was simply ignored by critics for many years. Natasha Marks, one of the few reviewers of his posthumous collection, *The Angel Horn*, asks in exasperation: 'Why the hell have I never read the work of this Vincentian poet before?'[20] Sara Florian, another critic of Anglophone Caribbean poetry, notes with more restraint the difficulty of finding critical material on his work.[21]

It is true that a number of his individual poems have been anthologised in collections both for adults and children, and their inclusion in the company of better known poets will have helped to keep his name before the poetry reading public.[22] However, apart from some limited literary criticism of his early writing, the incorporation of his work in doctoral theses by Veronica Austen and Sarah Florian, and my own essay published in *Small Axe*,[23] his work remains for the most part under-explored. In 2006 Veronica Austen drew attention to the way he uses the building blocks of language, particularly the way he manipulates the visual appearance of texts to represent sound on the page. Sarah Florian has discussed his 'creole aesthetics', his irreverent relationship with language and the ways he represents orality. So rather than being forgotten, his writing is today, perhaps, an open secret. At the same time, work has to be accessible before it can be criticised and this admittedly has been a problem for potential readers.

Ultimately, his work survives and serves the twenty-first century because of its underlying atmosphere of heady exuberance, rebellion and optimism, qualities he claimed were intrinsic to the West Indian writer. These are indeed the qualities of his poetry, which even in the darker moments of his life exude humour, optimism and flashes of joy. Unlike poets who have tried to represent jazz in their writing, Shake both played the music at a sophisticated level and used jazz forms in his poetry. Creating a jazz solo has much in common with writing a jazz poem. Both rely on improvisation, a skill not easily taught. Aspiring jazz musicians, whom Shake taught in his latter years, often asked him to teach them how to solo. His blunt answer was: 'If you want to solo listen to other musicians and copy them till you find your own way. There is no way to teach people to improvise, it's a contradiction in terms.'[24]

Shake was one of a group of virtuoso musicians who came together for a time, bringing new styles and ideas to a cooperative project of working out a range of riffs among themselves. As Ramanan notes, 'His technique and musical ear, honed by the militaristic training of his father, were exceptional. He had a unique style of phrasing that really reflected his puckish sense of humour.'[25] He makes the point also that Shake never really sounded like a conventional jazz musician. In Shake's last interview with David Austin before he died, Shake complimented the business acumen of younger jazz musicians but claimed that because their experience was more homogenised (presumably both in life and technique) they lacked a certain individuality that older musicians had. He summed it up in the statement. They are now 'too damn clean'.[26] Or, as he put it in one of his poems:

'Jazz, the Sane Man said,

tends to heal sweeter if the instruments
are not too sterilized.'[27]

As with his life, there is no easy conclusion to this discussion.

Notes

1. *Shake, Beat and Dub*, BBC TV, 1992.
2. For the full text of "Credential" see Appendix 3. In contrast, "Angel Horn," his final poem, offers a gentle summing up of the jazz man's life and was dedicated to both Coleridge Goode and Erik Bye, see Appendix 5.
3. Keane, *Collected Poems*, 91.
4. Val Wilmer, *Real Keen: Reggae into Jazz*, 1991, album sleeve notes.
5. Shake Keane, letter to John LaRose (nd, probably 1980).
6. Keane, *Collected Poems*, 91.
7. Keane, *Collected Poems*, 8.
8. Keane, *Collected Poems*, 8.
9. Keane, *Collected Poems*, 10.
10. Keane, *Collected Poems*, 14.
11. Keane, *OWWW*, 61.
12. Keane, *OWWW*, 63.

13 Keane, *OWWW*, 18.
14 Keane, *OWWW*, 15, 17, 19.
15 Keane, *OWWW*, 46.
16 Keane, *OWWW*, 49.
17 Keane, *OWWW*, 170.
18 Keane, *Collected Poems*, 79.
19 Keane, *Collected Poems*, 90.
20 Natasha C. Marks, "A Review of The Angel Horn - Shake Keane (1927-1997) Collected Poems," Moko Magazine, http://mokomagazine.org/wordpress/a-review-of-the-angel-horn-shake-kean-1927-1997-collected-poems/ accessed April 20, 2019.
21 Sara Florian, "Contemporary West Indian Poetry: a 'Creole' Aesthetics?" PhD. Sara Florian Tesi di dottorato 22 ciclo_2010 4 pdf, accessed March 10, 2019.
22 Paul Breman (ed), *You Better Believe It: Black Verse in English from Africa, the West Indies and the United States* (London: Penguin Books,1973); Paula Burnett (ed), *The Penguin Book of Caribbean Verse in English* (London: Penguin Classics, 1986); Stewart Brown and Ian McDonald (eds), T*he Heinemann Book of Caribbean Poetry* (London: Heinemann, 1992); Stewart Brown and Mark McWatt (eds), *The Oxford Book of Caribbean Verse (*Oxford: Oxford University Press, 2005).
23 Philip Nanton, "Shake Keane's 'Nonsense': An Alternative Approach to Caribbean Folk Culture," *Small Axe*, 14, September 2003, 71-92.
24 Austin, interview.
25 Ramanan, email correspondence.
26 Austin, interview.
27 Keane, *OWWW*, 19.

Shake outside Tiffany's Lounge, Bedford-Stuyvesant, Brooklyn, 1989. (*Val Wilmer*)

8/ THE VIEW FROM TIFFANY'S LOUNGE

In 1981 Shake once again left St Vincent, this time for New York. This second diaspora experience would turn out to be in dark contrast to the light of his earlier musical years in Britain and Europe.

On arrival in New York, he used the home of his older sister, Edna, as his mailing address; he may have stayed with her for a short time before renting a small room in an apartment building on St Mark's Avenue, Brooklyn. He then moved to 985 Bergen Street, a house divided into single rooms one of which he rented, in Bedford-Stuyvesant, the mainly Caribbean district of the city, busy and grubby with no shortage of 'Variety' stores. The house that he moved to was typical of many hundreds of such buildings, rundown brownstone tenements, with neighbours keeping themselves to themselves. The building was poorly maintained and with limited lighting which somehow spoke to his depressed mood. He captures the bleakness of his experience of New York in the sonnet 'Nostrand Avenue', written in 1982 soon after his arrival and which opens the collection *Brooklyn Themes*. The mood is conveyed in clipped, staccato sentences: 'The fall is here... Streets are scented with garbage. Young dangers roam.'

Dryly, he observes that:

here lost in a rented room
I must tackle the first inch of my current future.

Yet true to character, he adds a dash of dark humour:

Yesterday a cripple crossed
My way, inventing his every step. Had he not blocked
The view, I might have discovered (jesus christ) Brooklyn Bridge![1]

Christiane, with whom he remained in touch, soon became aware of his situation. When she called him from St Vincent, where she spent the Christmas of 1981 with his brother, Van, he was unable to hide his depression. On her return to London where she still lived, she wrote to his friends John LaRose and Sarah White expressing her concern: 'He is doing little — just gigs — and has no money.'[2]

At first, Shake found it difficult to resume his music career in New York because he did not have a work permit. But gradually unregistered work picked up in the form of transcribing music for bands, while he also obtained occasional studio work with calypsonians. He made recordings with a host of Caribbean musicians, including Vincentian soca artists Becket and Winston Soso, and Trinidadian calypsonians Duke, Calypso Rose and Chalkey. Frankie McIntosh, the New York-based Vincentian band leader and a close friend, saw much of Shake during these years. He recalled that when Shake first arrived they made plans for a variety of jazz-based recording projects, reprising some of the free form and jazz-and-poetry work that had found a following in Britain in the 1960s. However, McIntosh observed, musical tastes had shifted and as a producer, 'It was difficult to sell music with any substance or depth.'[3]

By this he meant modern jazz or anything other than popular forms. Circumstances were sufficiently difficult that, for a few years, Shake fell back on seasonal cruise ship gigs out of Miami.[4]

The problem of work limitations was not only a matter of being in the wrong place at the wrong time, Shake was also confronted by physical handicaps. Now aged 54, a knee injury, sustained as a youngster, along with the onset of gout, limited his mobility and his use of public transport. As a result he was restricted to walking around his neighbourhood. It was hardly surprising, then, that he fell back on his longstanding prop — alcohol.

Tiffany's Lounge, a bar on Nostrand Avenue, a block from his flat, became his second home. It was more than a place to hang out: the bar and its patrons were the inspiration for his last poetry collection, *Brooklyn Themes*, written between September 1982 and February 1983. According to the dedication, the Lounge regulars were his companions: 'For all my friends at the Tiffany's Lounge, Brooklyn, where all of these poems were conceived and most were written.'[5] Good friends from London occasionally visited. Val Wilmer recollected: 'Linton Johnson knew of my early friendship with Shake and even before he had been to Brooklyn to see Shake, he would discuss his hopes for a film whenever we met. Eventually he gave me Shake's address and telephone number and I contacted him the next time I was in New York. I went over to Bedford-Stuyvesant on several occasions and we'd meet for a Guinness with ice at Tiffany's Lounge on Nostrand Avenue.' This closer connection was a new experience for Wilmer. When she knew Shake in London, as she describes it, 'Ours was not a relationship of equals.' Younger than he was, Val had first met him through a mutual journalist friend, Kitty Grime. But when they met in New York he treated her more like an old friend and she found to her surprise, 'He was talking to me like an intellectual equal.' Their meetings whenever she was in New York became simply a bond of platonic friendship, and he was clearly pleased to see her on each visit. She recounted that as they chatted in the Lounge he would be greeted by others in the bar. He was sufficiently at home there to know the proprietor, Ruth Lloyd, and to introduce her to Wilmer.

Wilmer takes up the story: 'Tiffany's Cocktail Lounge was situated between a ladies' fashion shop and a liquor store at 625 Nostrand Avenue, the main thoroughfare, and less than half a mile from Shake's building. It was a small bar with a narrow shopfront, the room stretched backwards away from the street. It was typical of a thousand such watering-holes: low lighting, coloured bulbs to lend atmosphere, and a generous display of bottles piled up behind the bar. There was a barman to meet the customers' needs but, because I only went there in the late afternoon/early evening it seemed to be sparsely frequented. Some people sat at the bar on bar stools, we sat at one of the tables nearer to the entrance. There was a juke-box… and nothing remotely special about the place.'[6]

His loneliness and feeling of isolation was very apparent to her: 'Shake commented on some of his fellow drinkers and the neighbourhood people he knew. He explained that he had no cultural affinity with them. He was perfectly straightforward about this: they were people he'd drink with but in cultural terms they were poles apart. He lacked intellectual stimulation and he told me so. And that was why he was pleased to see me because I knew something of the world in which he'd lived in England. He mentioned other "foreigners" whose visits he anticipated with enthusiasm, but otherwise, he was stuck where he was, unable to move on because of his illegal status. He told me repeatedly of his frustration… he seemed to accept his situation, but he certainly wasn't happy about where he was living.'[7] I cite Wilmer's letter in detail as it paints a clear but depressing picture of Shake's situation and mood at the time.

Not surprisingly, the poems that he wrote around this time verge on the confessional. They support Wilmer's observations about his state of mind being shot through with bleakness, lacking any sense of movement or change. For example, 'The Bar' introduces a host of local Brooklyn characters, presumably regulars at Tiffany's Lounge: Scratch, Freckles, Dolores and Bowlegs (possibly nicknames bestowed by Shake) come, like him, to 'challenge' the bottles that face them on the shelf of the bar. When the bottles are empty they are replaced by new ones that look just the same — an image of stasis. Though most of the characters have a sad story to tell, any interaction between them is superficial. They use a language of mock politeness that hides the grim realities of their lives: 'How ya doon, honey — so they kill one another/To test their fear.'[8] This poem is a strong contrast to 'Roundtrip', an earlier and more up-beat poem about diaspora, partly set in a London pub. It is characterised by a sense of movement, change and community. Unlike those in 'The Bar', the characters in 'Roundtrip' become a family of sorts, learning to call each other "sister" and "brother". And the violence of his surroundings is captured in 'Love in Bed/Stuy — Brooklyn', a poem about the killing of a church minister in violent revenge for disowning a child he'd conceived with a member of his congregation.

In *Brooklyn Themes*, only in 'Sonnet for Margaret' do we glimpse any trace of hope or respite. After his arrival in New York, Shake reestablished contact with Margaret Bynoe, also from St Vincent, who had been a student at Bishop's College. Margaret, much younger than him, had left for New York to pursue graduate veterinary science studies, and would eventually hold a professorship at Cornell University. In New York, she and Shake established a relationship, and when the apartment where he was living was sold in 1991, they married and set up home together. The poem testifies to his love and appreciation for his younger wife:

*My dying would be truth if all my youth
Were recalled in you.*[9]

Later, the poem was included in *The Angel Horn: Collected Poems*, selected by Shake before he died. Margaret saw the book through to publication by House of Nehesi in 2005, and wrote a succinct afterword that summarised his achievements and captured his bleak New York situation. She wrote: 'In Brooklyn, he was unable to find immediate work because of his immigrant status and later admitted to feelings of alienation from his "rugged" Bedford-Stuyvesant neighbourhood.'[10] To ensure that his work reached a St Vincent public, Margaret organised a launch of his *Collected Poems* in the Peace Memorial Hall, Kingstown, in which I participated. She remained his partner until his death.

Despite the undoubted bond and mutual affection, their last years together would not have been easy. The reality of much of his time in New York found him out of touch with the roughness of Bedford-Stuyvesant life, frustrated by his illegal status and with limited opportunities to practise his art. When he visited London in 1988, and was interviewed by Peter Clayton, his voice is weary; he sounds dispirited. When he mentions his 'very minimal' New York life, Clayton, clearly disturbed by what he hears, says: 'Sounds like something of a waste of a man who I used to know.'[11] The interview begins to pick up a little only when Shake is encouraged to reflect if there was any value in his original migration to London. He mentions the importance of discovering the flugelhorn and playing with the

Joe Harriott Quintet.

There were other setbacks. He was twice mugged on the streets in New York at night while walking home from a gig. On one occasion, this resulted in a number of broken front teeth, a disaster for a trumpeter. Though he found he was able to play with dentures, Shake was never again satisfied with the sound he produced.

The picture then is of an isolated figure struggling for some equilibrium and in many ways out of touch with his environment, and aware that his high musical standards were beginning to suffer. Not the extreme circumstances of the American jazz men that Geoff Dyer sketches in *But Beautiful* but certainly moving in that direction. Shake had time on his hands and the desire for companionship at any time, particularly at night, deepened. Frankie McIntosh recollects long phone calls from him, 'quite often after 2.00am, to discuss a wide variety of topics, from the German philosopher Martin Heidegger to catching black fish in Barrouallie.'[12]

Other friends he had accumulated over the years in England and around the Caribbean also received periodic calls at unlikely times. Michael Garrick recollects: 'Once every few months the phone would ring, usually at three or four in the morning and his great voice would greet me, "Hello Michael, It's Shake. How you doin' man?"'[13] They could sense his feeling of exile and regret at such limited and occasional contact. He would phone novelist George Lamming, whom he had known at the BBC, partly to discuss Lamming's book *The Pleasures of Exile*. Though the book had been out a long time it had clearly resonated with him. For Lamming, these calls reflected Shake's nostalgia for the London of the 1950s and 1960s.[14] Adrian Fraser, another recipient of calls, observes: 'I got the impression that Shake was extremely lonely and not in the best of circumstances.'[15] Once a month he phoned Coleridge Goode in London.

From time to time, rays of light penetrated this gloom. Shake continued to travel and to play, returning sporadically to the itinerant musician's life he had led for so long. In 1989 he was invited to join the reconstituted Joe Harriott Memorial Quintet for a two-month tour of Britain. Re-formed by Michael Garrick, the band played Joe Harriott's arrangements. Along with Shake, the band members comprised Michael Garrick, Coleridge Goode, and Bobby Orr, who had played with the original Quintet. The alto saxophonist, Martin Hathaway, stood in for the late Joe Harriott. But this development was a mixed blessing. Both Shake's son Roland Ramanan and Goode noticed the fall off in his playing. Ramanan puts it like this: 'During those first concerts organised by Michael Garrick he was still capable of playing well, although dental problems limited him somewhat.'[16] Goode is more specific about the limitations. He noticed: 'Shake had become a pale shadow of his old musical self, his embouchure was in poor shape, his technique was hesitant and there were only rare hints of anything like the old brilliance.'[17]

Many of the late career opportunities that came his way were created by two friends: Linton Kwesi Johnson in London and Erik Bye in Norway. After the meeting at CARIFESTA in 1981, Johnson had for some time wanted to entice Shake to return to London to work, and would tell him this whenever he toured in New York and visited Shake there. This finally happened in 1991 when the programme *Shake, Beat and Dub* was made. The programme formed part of *Rhythms of the World*, BBC TV's award-winning documentary series, Arena. Johnson explained: 'When I heard he was coming to London in the early nineties I arranged for him to play on some tracks Dennis Bovell and I had composed. Then I arranged for him to play with the Dennis Bovell Dub band at the Ritzy in Brixton.... It was during that period Anthony [Wall] decided to make a documentary

Bassist Coleridge Goode, a close friend of Shake in his London days. (*Mary Dickinson*)

about him for Arena.'[18] The programme, directed by Mary Dickinson, captured something of Shake's and Linton's early years in their respective home islands of St Vincent and Jamaica. There are scenes of them performing independently and discussing their poetry with Michael Garrick and John LaRose. In the documentary, they also pay a visit to Coleridge Goode at his home in Notting Hill, London, where Shake had once lived, and he and Shake offer a taste of free form playing.

There are also film sequences of Linton and Shake walking slowly through the streets of London, with Shake reminiscing about old haunts — The Marquee, Flamingo and other clubs — locations that he once dominated. The ownership of London to which he lays claim in this sequence is in direct contrast with the disempowerment that he felt in New York. As they walk through Portobello Road, Johnson asks him about his memories of the street: 'Has it changed much?' Shake's reply is both jaunty and nostalgic. He answers: 'Well not really, not really at all. You could buy anything at half price (that) you could get anywhere else in London. This pub here now, The Duke of Wellington, used to be called Finches and this is where Coleridge Goode introduced me to a drink called Special Brew... we might go in...'[19] But they walk on.

In the previous year, backed by the Dennis Bovell Dub Band, Shake made *Real Keen: Reggae into Jazz*, an EP released under Linton Kwesi Johnson's LKJ label. He had suggested from time to time that this form of popular music was not his preferred genre. Nevertheless, on these tracks, as he plays and mixes it with the much younger reggae and dub musicians of the Band, his versatility shines through one last time.

From 1991, Shake went to Norway twice a year to play and to teach jazz workshops in Oslo and Bergen. The link with Norway came about with the revival of contact with Erik Bye, who had, like Shake, been employed as a producer at the BBC in London in the 1950s. By the 1990s, Bye had become a well-known popular ballad singer, television producer and philanthropist in Norway. Apart from arranging the jazz workshops, Bye secured gigs for Shake at a variety of venues around the country. These included cathedrals, an oil drilling platform, theatres and jazz cafes. He also resolved Shake's costly needs in terms of health checks, which had become an element in his visits, and, in one instance, new dentures, by incorporating these costs into the terms for his appearances.[20]

Shake outside the BBC's Bush House, London, with poet and musician Linton Kwesi Johnson, 1992 (*Mary Dickinson*)

Posters for Oslo Jazz Festival where Shake played in 1991 and 1992. (*Courtesy Sue Walcott*)

In Norway, Shake also acted — as Ellsworth Keane — in a Norwegian television documentary series, *The Search for Mangas Coloradas* (1992-1993), about the life of the nineteenth-century Apache chief of the same name. Though activities like these were occasional, they offered a respite from the harsher circumstances of his New York life. Bye had wanted to visit St Vincent and to see the homeland of one of his best friends — and who better to show him around? But Shake always demurred. 'There was a wound there,' said Bye.[21]

In 1997, Bye invited Shake to do one more jazz tour to Norway. By then, however, Shake was suffering from stomach cancer, which had spread to the bone marrow. Though he was losing weight, he kept this development to himself as he was determined to fulfil the arrangement with his friend. Given the state of his health he knew that he was near the end and believed that Erik and his family would look after him. Erik was shocked when Shake arrived off the plane in a wheelchair, a thin replica of himself. But Shake had one last job to do — reading a poem for broadcast. Erik had to do it for him while Shake watched from his hospital bed —and criticised Erik for his 'lack of idiom'. He died on 11 November at Det Norske Radium hospital in Oslo holding Erik's hand.

On 22 November his funeral and cremation was held in Norway, organised by Erik as a last act of friendship. The ceremony included live jazz performances while 'Abide with me', one of Shake's favourite hymns, was sung in Norwegian and English. He was 70. It was then that Roland Ramanan discovered how important Shake had become to Bye. 'I was astounded by the love expressed for Shake by Erik's whole extended family.' Shake had once requested to Bye that his ashes be scattered in the sea off Norway; they were, in fact, returned to St Vincent.

Shake led a rich and varied artistic life with high levels of accomplishment in both literature and music. But in his story the relationship between art and life is a complicated one. He was acclaimed in the international world of jazz as well as Caribbean poetry circles, and, however briefly, reached the upper echelons of his island's official world. By contrast, he had also experienced a troubled reception back in St Vincent and the difficulties of a second diaspora experience — in a way, a self-imposed exile — in New York. He was undoubtedly more at home in the informal world of music and performance than the formal world of government. But, despite setbacks in both, he endured and made his mark, carving out a life of relative artistic freedom on his own terms. What this phrase signifies is a commitment to collaboration in the making of music of all kinds — from simple to complex; a commitment to his own way of living his life, whatever the cost; and third, a commitment to

Shake with Erik Bye, the Norwegian producer and promoter, who looked after Shake during the final days of his life. (*Courtesy Roland Ramanan*)

challenging the conventional boundary between playing jazz and writing poetry.

As a Caribbean migrant musician in post-war London, he is also part of a history that demands to be remembered and is slowly being uncovered. He features in Alan Robertson's biography *Joe Harriott: Fire In His Soul* and in the respective autobiographies of Coleridge Goode, Michael Garrick and Jeremy Robson. Each one pays fulsome tributes to Shake's musicianship. In his autobiography, Garrick is unstinting in his praise of both Joe Harriott and Shake. He observed: 'Joe and Shake scaled the heights in the beauty and originality of their playing, which made their personal decline all the more tragic… I see them as the nearest equivalent to Diz and Bird the UK ever produced.'[22] Many of the recordings of the Joe Harriott Quintet have been revived, as have *Jazz Praises* as well as poetry and jazz recordings that Shake and Joe made with Michael Garrick and Jeremy Robson.[23] In 2007 the jazz critic, Kevin Le Gendre, singled out the Quintet's *Free Form* as 'one of the great jazz albums of the last five decades.'[24]

How does his son, Roland Ramanan, as a contemporary jazz musician in England, see Shake's legacy? His response: 'Shake left little behind in comparison to his enormous talent. Very few recordings really do him justice. He left behind few written compositions... The Caribbean London-based flautist and composer Rowland Sutherland wanted to honour Shake by playing one of his tunes from the record 'In My Condition'. Unfortunately, the copy they had mislabelled tracks and they later discovered they had learnt the wrong tune — it was a cover of a song by a completely different artist. I think Shake would have found this very funny. It does also show that Shake is being picked up by young black players in the UK who are interested in the legacy of the pioneers who went before them. They are much more conscious of what it means to be a black artist.'[25]

After he died, newspaper obituaries in London, New York and St Vincent extolled Shake's achievements. As *The Times* put it: 'The most brilliant trumpeter and flugelhorn player of his generation of London-based West Indian musicians, he was also a prize winning poet and an educator.'[26] One Vincentian newspaper claimed that he was 'a great Vincentian... perhaps better known internationally than in the country in which he was born.'[27] Soon after his death, a sparsely attended memorial service was held for him in the Kingstown Methodist Church.

A few years passed. The political regime that had dismissed him from his post as Director of Culture was again in power. But Shake's stature as an international artist was undeniable. The world had praised his musicianship, and his home country could not deny the accolades. Pressure mounted for an official response. A bust of Shake Keane was commissioned and in a few years a dark, polished wooden bust, with spectacles, was duly completed.

The unveiling was an official affair at which I was invited to speak. It was held in Kingstown's art centre, the Peace Memorial Hall. I expected a substantial audience, but it was held during the day which limited the numbers. Time had passed and musical tastes had changed. There was a small table in a plain room from which a minister of government and a few others, including myself, looked out onto a sparse audience. When it was my time to speak I suggested that Shake's achievements were heroic. Afterwards, the minister took me aside and pointed out that Shake was not an official National Hero. That accolade requires formal government Cabinet approval. There is one officially recognised national hero in St Vincent, Chief Joseph Chatoyer, the French-speaking Carib who resisted the British in the eighteenth century. Shake clearly did not match up. Had he been present I could imagine a wry smile. With typical irony he once observed to his friend Erik Bye: 'When you're dead you're famous.'[28]

Notes

1 Keane, *Collected Poems*, 165.
2 Christiane Keane, letter to John LaRose and Sarah White, nd circa 1982.
3 Frankie McIntosh, email to Adrian Fraser, November 19, 1997.
4 Larry Brown Jr., email correspondence with the author, July 16, 2020.
5 Keane, *Collected Poems*, 163.
6 Val Wilmer, letter to author, February 12, 2020.
7 Wilmer, letter.
8 Keane, *Collected Poems*, 175.
9 Keane, *Collected Poems*, 169.
10 Margaret Bynoe, "About the Author," *Collected Poems*, 183-184.
11 Clayton, interview.

THE VIEW FROM TIFFANY'S LOUNGE

12 McIntosh, email to Adrian Fraser.
13 Garrick, *Dusk Fire*, 64.
14 'I think he has been feeling a very keen nostalgia for the period of the London sojourn of the 50's and 60's which that book records.' George Lamming to Adrian Fraser, correspondence February 8, 1996.
15 Adrian Fraser, *Searchlight*, St Vincent, November 12, 1999.
16 Ramanan, email correspondence.
17 Goode, *Bass Lines*, chapter 9, para 32, Kindle.
18 Linton Kwesi Johnson, email to the author, May 23, 2019.
19 *Shake, Beat and Dub,* BBC TV, 1992.
20 Bye fondly remembered how, on one visit, they had to send a taxi to fetch Shake's dentures so he could make music.
21 Erik Bye, interview by the author, "Angel Horn", BBC Radio 3, December 15, 2002.
22 Garrick, *Dusk Fire*, 67.
23 See selected discography. A Facebook page dedicated to Shake containing background information and photographs can be seen at https://www.facebook.com/PoetryIntoJazz/.
24 Kevin Le Gendre, "Joe Harriott Quintet - Free Form," *Jazzwise*, October 4, 2007. https://www.jazzwise.com/review/article/joe-harriott-quintet-free-form.
25 Ramanan, email correspondence.
26 *The Times*, "Shake Keane," obituary, November 28, 1997.
27 Blazer C Williams, "Ellsworth McGranahan 'Shake' Keane," *The News*, November 14, 1997, 6.
28 Bye, BBC Radio 3, 2002.

APPENDIX/1

Part of this poem forms the epigram that opens Chapter 5 and is among a number of Shake's unpublished poems. This poem was given to the author by the late Christiane Keane.

On A Plane

PEOPLE sit at windows
And they look
Inwards
    Courtesy is a duty-free need
    Drinking is an obligation recycled
Like breathing.....

    The bird shudders

The bird
    Heavier than mud - A mega-pregnancy
        Lighter than mountains
Migrates through the night.....
Sleep is an obligation
    A flight into winter
        For birds far from natural

Until the last hour
Windows bring nothing into sight....

And I
Lighter than the earth
heavier than mud
Have flown too far north

Far too far north
From home.

(Keane, 28 January 1992)

APPENDIX/2

Below is the full text of an early poem part of which is cited in Chapter 6. The poem betrays strong Christian influences. It formed one of Shake's offerings to the BBC *Caribbean Voices* radio programme and was attached to correspondence with Cyril Cyrus (25 November 1950). The correspondence and poem were given to the author by Cecil Cyrus in 2001.

Recitative for Christmas

"Oh Jerusalem, hadst thou but known."

And this man I met
Took me down beside the still mist
Beyond Bethlehem. Beside the mist
And the quiet waters and the dumb pastures,
And in the morning, in the lisp
Of the young wind, he set
Me down,
Beyond babble of Bethlehem's two thousand futures,
This man I met.
     And weeping, he said,
I was born there, yesterday,
Long ago, under doom
Of a thousand prophesies,
There in the heart of that solemn clay
Was I born, issue
Of the hand whose and whom
I am. For I am also he
Who flamed in the bush for a token
And in the sky for a covenant
And in two walled sins
Down in the plain of the pillar of salt...
There in the heart of that clay

RIFF

I have always been born.

Oh Caribbean, hadst thou but known....

*And because he had heard my sighing
I told him.
I told him of my birth years ago in a land
Where they had saved souls and sold slaves
In the completion and the denying
Of one decree.
And how they had fled in ships
From hot Sodoms, like birds,
As sometimes there in September we see them,
Ripping the cold air with wings,
When the thunder gargles whole showers
And heaven breaks out in sores.*

*I would have told him too
Of hunger and of the horror,
Death and the corruption of faith.
But the wind rose, and the mist
Came upon me in a thousand crowded tears,
And I saw that my own faith
Was a pillared woman, gazing
Backward
Over the wreck of the flamed plain,
With eyes vacant as salt.*

Oh Jerusalem, could'st thou have known?

*And this man I met
Down by the mist in the young wind
Had spoken again,
Now about a hand that had broken a tomb*

And stroked his eyes with resurrection -
And it was the Hand whose and whom
He was.
And he spoke two thousand years in one song.
And it was a simple song
And it was a subtle song
And it was a dreadful song
And it was a delicate song
As you might hear sometimes in April
When the sea is in a coma
And a neat nurse of a wind
Gathers surf gently like a sheet
Over the soft shoulders of sand,
And putters around the stiff palms
Humming idly...
It was the kind of song you felt you'd heard before,
And lost, and found, only to loose and find again
Like the memory of your first love
Or your father's dying words.

Oh Jerusalem, Oh Caribbean, hast thou not known?

It spoke as the sea churned
And the sky bled
And the valley flamed
And the mist went somersaulting mad
Down the hillside like swine into negation...
Over the churn of the rain and the rolling mist
It spoke of love, tall as mountains,
And toil
And passion like a young shoot
Knowing the ecstasy of the new sun...
And so, forth from the wall of a thousand tears
Forth from the call of mist

RIFF

And the young wind lisping
Beside dumb pastures, and the call
Of the dead pillar in the plain,
We went,
Into the moment of tall mountains,
Beyond babble of Bethlehem's two thousand futures.

(Keane, 8 October 1950.)

APPENDIX/3

This is the full text of Shake's poem that responds to his sense of rejection on his return to St Vincent.

Lesson Seven: CREDENTIAL.
(for Shadow, a modern kaisonian)

SIX year ole
an' me farder gimme a trumpit
an' 'e show me
how to blow it
how to polish it
How to respec' it
An 'e say

                        exercise yo potential
Hold on to dis

But de neighbour-dem say
Bwoy wheh yo manners
Wheh yo wool-tie
Wheh yo hymnbook an' yo cork-hat
Yo mean yo farder didn't gie yo dat?...

           So Ah try out me credential
           Ah tek it out
           an' Ah polish it
           an' dey like it
           an' Ah say
           Me farder didn' gie me dat
           But 'e gimme dis

Eighteen year ole
An' me girlfrien' vex wid me trumpit
She say

RIFF

> *bwoy wheh you money*
Wheh yo hard-pants
Wheh yo whisky and yo shut-jack an yo Fiat
dat is essential
udderwise you gwine miss

> *tit fe tat*

> *So Ah roll-up me credential*
> *We repolish it*
> *Then Ah **blow-it***
> *An' she like it*
> *An' Ah say*
> *Me farder didn' gimme dat*
> *But 'c gie we*
> *Dis*

Twenty-five year ole
An' Ah hit de mudder-country
An' Ah show dem all me manners and me certifikiss
But de trouble me
She

> *Bwoy wheh yo histry*
> *where your culture*
> *where your farder*
> *wheh yo money and yo hot-shirt*
> *wheh yo felt-hat.....*

Ah say no profit no potential in dis
So Ah tek out me essential
an' Ah polish it

> **an' dey respec' it**
> **An' So dey respec' it So Ah blow it**
> **An' Ah say**

> ***Is me farder wha' gimme dat***
> ***An' wha' gimme***
> ***Dis***

Forty year ole
an' Ah touch back down pon me country
an' Ah like it
an' Ah cool it
an' Ah bring back all me farder trumpit
gie dem

But de sweet fool-dem say
> *Bwoy **What** yo come home for*
wheh yo big car
wheh yo wool-hat
wheh yo snap-soul an' yo whiskey an' yo 'tankerousniss
All-we culture all-we potential
Is definightly non-residential
All dis trumpit is a famous load o'piss

> *hold on to dis*

> *So Ah hice up me credential*
> *same one wha' me farder show*
> *how fe polish*
> *how fe respec'*
> *how fe blow*
> *An' Ah say..// 3/4!Sxhf=+f@@@...*

(St Vincent, 25 June 1976)

APPENDIX/4

This unpublished poem celebrates Shake Keane's grandson. It appears in a hand-written form on his Facebook page; and was also spoken by Shake in the TV programme, *Brixton to Barbados*.

First and Last Birthday Poem
(for my grandson - Thomas, 1990)

As a baby he would shake hands
With anything, the unknown X
Between the breasts of female wellwishers,
His godfather's forefinger, even the thrust
Of fear from a sudden shout.
It was a useful reflex,
Like smiling when in doubt.

Later he would learn, even invent, brands
of rejection, need, confusion, tentative denials,
Racial subtleties, international locks,
Symbols wrestled out of wrists and thumbs,
Five-fingered inflections, precise as rubbing noses,
or, in seclusion, trials
Of more private digital poses.

And in all these song scattering years never a demand
from his right fist to know the truth, -
how so much erudition could accrue
from the simple contagion of experience.
the rage to know and to avoid.
Born wrong-handed, fear-conditioned, shrewd,
He may nevertheless exchange whole harvests of youth
for a fistful of arthritic attitudes....

Now, old as truth, he shakes his own hands,

APPENDICES

landlocked, unaware of sequences or sexes,
eyes uninflected like an arrival endlessly foretold,
fists shrivelled like a thousand subtleties,
Mouth mute, hygienic, like a doll's mouth, DASH
The sum of all his reflexes,
Smiling always,

    No doubt.

APPENDIX/5

The full text of Shake's final poem dedicated to Coleridge Goode and Erik Bye.

Angel Horn

When I was born
My father gave to me
an angelhorn
With wings of melody.
That angel placed her lips
upon my finger-tips
and I became, became
her secret name.

Her name grew strong,
spread like a passion tree.
She named the song,
I played the melody.
And in the morning hour
I awoke to dream of her,
And all day long, day long
I lived her song.

In boat and barge
where songs and seas are friends
our dreams grew large,
made love where dreaming ends.
And people placed her lips
upon our finger-tips,
and friends became, became
our secret name.

APPENDICES

Now light is low,
new angels come and go.
The passion tree
Spreads dense as destiny.
And this old angelhorn
strives like the lifting dawn!
Love moves to claim,
to claim our secret name.

(Keane, *Collected Poems*, 181-182)

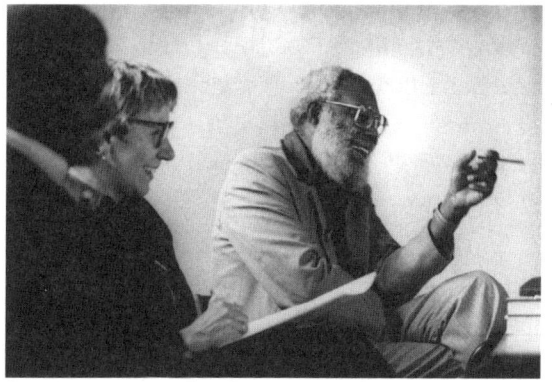

Jamaican trumpeter Pete Pitterson joins Shake Keane for 'Bebop and Beyond', a National Sound Archive discussion chaired by Val Wilmer (centre) at the Africa Centre, London, 1989. (*Melanie Friend*)

DISCOGRAPHY

Shake Keane's discography contains 158 recordings divided into Releases (18), Appearances (26) and Credits (114). The full listing can be found at www.discogs.com>artist>475808-Shake Keane. This selected listing demonstrates his range of recordings comprising albums, singles and EPs, compilations as well as selected recordings with European big bands and Caribbean artists.

Albums
Dannie Abse, Laurie Lee, Adrian Mitchell, Jeremy Robson, The Michael Garrick Quintet featuring Joe Harriott and Shake Keane, *Poetry and Jazz in Concert*, Record One and Record Two (mono) Argo, US, 1964.

Michael Garrick Quintet featuring Joe Harriott and Shake Keane, *October Woman*, Argo, US, 1965; Vocalion, UK, 2005 (also CD).

Shake Keane With The Keating Sound, *Shake Keane With The Keating Sound*, Decca, UK, 1965; London Records, UK and US, 1966.

Shake Keane, *That's The Noise*, Ace of Clubs, UK, 1967; Vocalion, UK, 2005.

Shake Keane, *Dig It!*, Decca, UK, 1969; London Records, Canada, US, 1969; Decca, Germany, nd.

Shake Keane, The Kilimanjaro Strings and Orchestra, The Hastings Girls Choir, *Rising Stars at Evening Time*, Pama Records, UK, 1970.

Shake Keane, *Real Keen: Reggae into Jazz*, LKJ Records, UK, 1991 (also CD).

Albums with Joe Harriott Quintet
Joe Harriott Quintet and Sextet, *Southern Horizons*, Jazzland, US and Europe, 1960, Down at Dawn, 2013 and 2020.

Harriott Quintet, *Free Form*, Jazzland, US and Europe, 1961; EmArcy, UK and Europe, 1988, also CD; Gott Discs, UK, 2007; Doxy, Europe, 2014, also CD; Jazz Workshop, Spain, 2018.

The Joe Harriott Quintet, *Abstract*, Columbia, 1963, Capitol Records, US,

1963; EmArcy, UK and Europe 1998 (also CD); Doxy, Europe, 2014; Jazz Workshop, Spain, 2014.

Joe Harriott Quintet, *High Spirits*, Lansdown Series, Columbia, UK, 1965.

The Joe Harriott Quintet, *Movement*, Columbia, UK, 1964.

Singles and EPs

The Joe Harriott Quintet, *A Guy Called Joe*, Lansdown Series, Columbia, UK, 1961, EP.

Shake Keane Quintet, *In My Condition*, Columbia, UK, 1961, EP.

Jeremy Robson with The Michael Garrick Trio and Joe Harriott and Shake Keane, *Blues for the Lonely*, Lansdown Series, Columbia, UK, 1963, EP.

Shake Keane and the Boss Men, *Bossa Negra*, Lansdown Series, Columbia, UK, 1963, EP.

Shake Keane, The Hastings Girls Choir, The Gordon Langford Orchestra, *Rising Star*, Airborne Records, UK, 1964, EP.

Shake Keane and the Michael Garrick Quartette, *A Case of Jazz,* Airborne Records, UK, 1964, EP.

Shake Keane, *Calle Washington*, Airborne Records, UK, 1964, single.

Michael Garrick Quintet with Shake Keane and Joe Harriott, *Anthem*, Argo, US, 1965, EP.

Shake Keane, *Soul Serenade/Green Onions*, Decca, Netherlands, 1969, single.

Compilations

Caribbean Connections, Black Music in Britain in the Early 1950s, Volume 2, New Cross Records, UK, 1987.

Shake Keane, *Dig It!/Shake Keane with the Keating Sound*, Vocalion, UK, 2005.

Michael Garrick and Shake Keane, *Rising Stars*, Trunk Records, 2011.

Selected recordings with European-based big bands

Jonny Teupen, *Love and Harp A La Latin*, Vogue Schallplatten, 1965; Sonorama, Germany, 2008, album.

Carl Drevo Und Die Clarke-Boland Big Band, *Swing, Waltz, Swing*, Phillips, 1966; Rearward, Italy, 2008, album.

The Kenny Clarke-Francy Boland Big Band, *Sax No End*, SABA, Germany, 1967, album.

Kurt Edelhagen Und Seine All-Star-Band, *Jazz Im WDR*, Neuphone Records, Germany, 1967, album.

Charly Antolini, *Soul Beat*, MPS Records, Germany, 1968, album.

OG Blarr, Ursula Terhoeven, Chor Der Neanderkirche Dusseldorf, *Denn-Er-Hat Wunder Getan*, Schwann AMS Studio, Germany, 1968, album.

Jonny Teupen, *Harpadelic*, MPS Records, Germany, 1969; Japan, 1999; Germany, 2014, album.

Kurt Edelhagen and His Orchestra, *Kurt Edelhagen Plays Jim Webb*, Polydor, Germany, 1972, album.

J Teupen, JA Rettenbacher, *XX Olympiade Munchen 1972*, KTS, Germany, 1972, single.

Kenny Clarke, Francy Boland, *Ebullient, Roaring, Screaming Big Band Sound*, BASF, MPS Records, Germany, 1972, album.

Das Orchester Kurt Edelhagen, *Jazz/Pop*, Westdeutscher Rundfunk, Germany, 1972, album.

Sincerely P.T., *Sincerely PT*, Spiegelei, Germany, 1973, album.

Sincerely P.T., *Fresh Air Where?/Rolling Machine*, Spiegelei, Germany, 1973, single.

Selected recordings with Caribbean artists

Poser, *Hot and Sweet*, Rohit International, Russ Dev Ltd, Jamaica/US, 1983, album.

Becket, *Vincy Mas*, Cocoa Records, US, 1983, album.

Sparrow, *King of the World*, Dynamic Sounds, Jamaica; B's Records, US, 1984, album.

Explainer, *The Awakening*, B's Records, US, 1984, album.
Zero (56), *Extra Special*, Veebee Records, Antigua & Barbuda, 1984, album.
Becket, *10th Anniversary,* Cocoa Records, US, 1985, album.
Tommy T, *I Wanna Make Love*, Lem's Records, US, 1987, mini album.
King Short Shirt, *25th Anniversary*, WB Records, US, 1987, album.
Becket, *Soca Dance Party*, Cocoa Records, US, 1988, album.
Gypsy, *Life*, MRS Records, US, 1988, album.
Destroyer, *Twice As Bad*, Guy Records, Canada, 1988, album.
Lady Pearl, *Beautiful*, Secko Music, Canada, 1989, 12".
Ajamu, *Don't Spoil It*, All-J Heavyweight Productions, US, 1989, album.

Selected Highlife Recordings
Shake Keane with the Highlifers, *Trumpet Highlife,* Lyragon, UK, 1954, 10".
Ambrose Campbell, *High Life Today*, Columbia, UK, 1966, album.

BIBLIOGRAPHY

Austen, Veronica J, "Inhabiting the Page: Visual Experimentation in Caribbean Poetry," unpublished thesis, Ontario, University of Waterloo, 2006.

Baugh, Edward, "West Indian Poetry 1900-1970: A Study in Cultural Decolonisation", Savacou Pamphlet no1, Mona, *Savacou* Publications, 1971.

"Department of Culture: Projects, Priorities, Plans 1974/75," unpublished, Kingstown, St Vincent.

Dyer, Geoff, *But Beautiful: A Book About Jazz,* New York, North Point Press/Farrar, Straus & Giroux, 1996.

Florian, Sara, "Contemporary West Indian Poetry: a 'Creole' Aesthetics?", PhD. Ca Foscari University of Venice, 2010.

Fraser, Adrian. *The 1935 Riots in St Vincent: From Riots to Adult Suffrage*, Kingston, University of the West Indies Press, 2016.

Garrick, Michael with Trevor Bannister, *Dusk Fire: Jazz in English Hands*, Reading, Springdale Publishing, 2010.

Goode, Coleridge and Roger Cotterrell, *Bass Lines: A Life in Jazz*, London, Northway, 2002.

Hobsbawm, Eric, *The Jazz Scene*, London, Faber and Faber, 1992.

Mitchell, James, *Beyond the Islands: An Autobiography,* Oxford, Macmillan Caribbean, 2006.

Moore, Hilary, *Inside British Jazz: Crossing Borders of Race, Nation and Class*, Aldershot, Ashgate, 2007.

Robertson, Alan, *Joe Harriott: Fire in His Soul*, London, Northway Publications, 2011.

Robson, Jeremy, *Under Cover. A Poet's Life in Publishing…And All That Jazz*, Hull, Biteback Publishing, 2018.

Rohlehr, Gordon, "The Problem of the Problem of Form" in *The Shape of that Hurt and Other Essays,* Port of Spain, Longman, 1992.

Walcott, Derek, *Derek Walcott - Collected Poems 1948-1984*, London, Faber and Faber, 1992.

Walter, Robert, *The Yearbook of the Bermudas, The Bahamas, British Guiana, British Honduras and the British West Indies*, Canada Gazette Ltd, 1928.

Wilmer Val, "Ellsworth McGranahan (Shake) Keane (1927-1997), Jazz Musician and Poet," *Oxford Dictionary of National Biography*, Oxford, Oxford University Press, 2004.

Wilmer Val, *As Serious as Your Life: The Story of the New Jazz*, London, Allison and Busby, 1977.

Wilmer, Val, *Mama Said There'd Be Days Like This: My Life in the Jazz World*, London, Women's Press, 1989.

SHAKE KEANE PUBLICATIONS

L'Oubli: Poems, The Author, Bridgetown, Barbados Advocate, 1950.

Ixion: Poems, Miniature Poets no. 10, Georgetown, (British) Guiana, 1952.

Nancitori With Drums, The Author, Reliance Printery, Kingstown, 1972.

One A Week With Water: Rhymes and Notes, Ediciones Casa de las Américas, Havana, 1979.

The Volcano Suite: A Series of Five Poems, The Author, Fishnet Restaurant, Kingstown, 1979.

Brooklyn Themes: Poems, September 1982-February 1983, The Author, New York, 1983.

Palm and Octopus: Twelve Love Poems, The Author, New York, 1994.

The Angel Horn: Shake Keane Collected Poems (1927-1997)*, House of Nehesi, Philipsburg, St Maarten, 2005.

---

*Two unpublished collections of poems "Thirteen Studies in Home Economics" (St Vincent 1972-1977) and "The Wisdom Keepers" (St Vincent 1972-1974) were incorporated in Collected Poems, 2005.

ACKNOWLEDGEMENTS

A biography about an international jazz figure like Shake Keane, who comes from a small place, offers an opportunity to get to know better both the person and the place. It offers the chance to explore and discover aspects of that society through the life of a complex person. A biography entails opening up an intimate history. By the term 'intimate history' I mean not only an emotional life fully lived but also that Shake was someone to whom some in St Vincent society felt a strong attachment; not least because of the fame by osmosis that his international achievements offered the country.

I must begin with one admission. In the opening sketch to this book I fictionalised the name of the bar and the owner. The event I describe did happen at the location I identified. While I do remember the event as one of our first meetings I never remembered the name of the person who ran the bar, the name of the bar nor the person who entered and offered to sing for Shake. I never dreamed that I would be writing Shake Keane's biography. The sketch is there simply to illustrate his informal but widespread appeal in the island at that time. All other events and situations that I recount are supported with evidence and references where possible.

My short biography of Shake Keane focuses on the man and the context in which he lived in the twentieth century. Though I am a jazz lover I am not an expert, and so cannot speak with authority on the intricacies of his musical talent and the details of free form jazz and the other music idioms in which he excelled. My aim has been to tell the story of the challenges that Shake faced, the life that he lived, often expressed through his writing, and to show the extent to which he overcame these challenges. Over the years and in the course of my research I've talked to many people about Shake and his achievements and I'd like to record my thanks to those who have knowingly and unknowingly helped me construct this biography.

In the course of my research it was my good fortune that H. Nigel Thomas introduced me to David Austin who coincidentally was visiting Barbados while I was preparing this biography. David kindly made available a long interview that he had conducted with Shake in New York a few years before Shake died. I mined this interview intensely and I am grateful for David's willingness to share the contents with me.

Cheryl King, through her extensive email network of Vincentians at home and abroad, kindly put out a request for help on my behalf when I wanted it known that I was working on Shake's biography. This led to a full interview with Sir James Mitchell in Bequia who allowed me access to his memories and the files that he kept about his friend Shake. Through the link with Cheryl King, Fred Prescod and others provided helpful reminiscences of early St Vincent that I could draw on. On a visit to St Vincent I held a long phone conversation with the journalist Bassy Alexander whose recollections created a vivid picture of early Kingstown where Shake lived in his formative years.

Adrian Fraser kindly allowed me access to a short encomium by Errol King on Shake's early achievements in St Vincent. Shake was being honoured as a 'Senior Citizen of Culture' on 27 October 1996 by the New York Council of St Vincent and the Grenadines. Through Adrian's link with the Vincentian musician Frankie McIntosh I got to know something about Shake's later life in New York.

The jazz critic John Stephenson introduced me to Roland Ramanan, who patiently, fully and carefully answered my many questions about Shake from the perspective of both a son living in England and a practising jazz musician.

Many years ago I had a chance meeting with Alan Robertson when he was researching his biography, *Joe Harriott, Fire in His Soul*. We discussed the idea of a study of Shake but again I never thought that I would be the person to write one. Alan's biography, along with the autobiographies by Coleridge Goode and Michael Garrick, have been important in helping me understand Shake in the milieu of jazz musicians of the 1960s with whom he mixed. Alan also provided me with access to a BBC interview that Shake gave to Peter Clayton on *Sounds of Jazz* in 1988.

I have drawn on the jazz historian Val Wilmer's detailed knowledge of the British jazz scene and Shake's role in it. We have corresponded a number of times and I have relied on Val's shrewd observations in those letters, her well-documented interviews with him both in London and New York and her Guardian obituary: *Shake Keane: The Anger Behind a Free Form of Jazz* (Wilmer, 1997). With considerable patience Val has also pointed out a number of my more glaring errors and inconsistencies in an early draft of the manuscript. She has kindly allowed use of the photograph on the cover and some of those in the text of this book. I have dedicated this book to her.

In the latter stages of the writing it was my good luck to make contact with the poet and publisher Jeremy Robson. His intimate knowledge of the poetry and jazz scene in England of the 1960s and his helpful interventions greatly enhanced my understanding of that history and Shake's role in it.

In the early 2000s I interviewed Christiane Keane, Coleridge Goode, Michael Garrick and Val Wilmer in London; Edgar Adams and Cecil Cyrus in St Vincent and Erik Bye (by telephone) in Norway. These interviews contributed to the making of a BBC Radio 3 programme on Shake, *Angel Horn*, which I researched and presented. It was first broadcast December 15 2002. Listening again to the full interviews was especially helpful when I returned to immerse myself in his story.

I met Professor Margaret Bynoe in 2006 at the launch of Shake's *The Angel Horn: Collected Poems 1927-1997* in Kingstown when she encouraged my critical analysis of Shake's poetry. She expressed her support for a radio programme and essay of mine when I spoke at the book launch she held in Kingstown for his *Collected Poems*. Despite a number of attempts, including through House of Nehesi Publishers, regrettably I was unable to establish contact with her with regard to this book. I am grateful to Lasana M. Sekou, publisher at House of Nehesi, for kindly allowing the reproduction on page 94 of the cover art image 'S Keane' 2004, charcoal by Joe Dominique, of *Collected Poems* as well as for the reproduction of a number of poems identified in the text.

Jonelle Williams helped me negotiate the Public Records Office in Kingstown.

Linton Kwesi Johnson responded quickly and helpfully to my questions about his friendship and working relationship with Shake.

A chance moment of googling led me to the archivist Sarah Garrod based at the George Padmore Institute in London. She kindly provided me with access to correspondence between John LaRose, Shake and Christiane Keane.

In the West Indian Collection of the Sidney Martin Library at University of The West Indies, Cave Hill Campus, Barbados, I was able to read Shake's first two poetry collections and his essays and occasional poems published in the early issues of *Bim* magazine.

My early drafts were cautious and constricted. My partner Jane Bryce helped me polish the work into a more free-flowing story. But all errors, faults and shortcomings in this work remain my own.

This is the third book I have published with Papillote Press. Without the editorial skill and perspicacious interrogation of Polly Pattullo and Andy Dark's designer skills this one would have fallen far short of what it is. Polly's passion for Caribbean stories is only equalled by her professionalism and commitment to the highest standards.

INDEX

Abse, Dannie, 55
Adaha, 34
Adams, Edgar, 75, 149
Advocate Company, 23
African-American, 62
alcohol, 84, 113
Alexander, Bassy, 148
All Stars, *see* Harlem All Stars
Alpha Boys' School, 61
American, 8, 13, 31, 32, 60, 117
Amerindian, 98
Anancy stories, 16
Angel Horn (BBC programme), 65
　Angel Horn The: Collected Poems, 82, 104–5, 116, 149.
Angel Horn (poem), 138
Anglo-Ashanti War, 34
Antolini, Charly, 62
Aquatic Club, 76
Arena, 118, 119
Argo, 55
Armstrong, Louis, 13, 31
Associated Statehood, 4
Austen, Veronica, 106
Austin, David, 57, 107, 148

Ballwin, James, 98
Barbados, 8, 20, 23, 27, 29, 78–9, 148, 150
Barber, Chris, 32
Barnes, Colin, 55
Barrouallie, 15, 78, 88, 117
Baugh, Edward, 87
BBC, 20, 27–9, 39–40, 54, 65, 95, 117–18, 120–1, 129, 149

Becket, 112
Beckett, Harry, 35
Bedford-Stuyvesant, 110–11, 113, 116
Beglan, Dan, 88
Bequia, 17, 74, 148
Bergen, 111, 120
Bible, 14, 84–5
Bim, 20–1, 53, 83, 85, 150
Bishop's College, 2, 75, 89, 115
Blarr, Oskar Gottlieb, 62
Boland, Francy, 62
bossa nova, 35
Bovell, Dennis, 118, 120
Boyea, Willy, 15
Boys' Grammar School (BGS), 14, 16–18, 32, 74
brass band, 12–13, 15
Brathwaite, Edward 'Kamau', 29, 87, 100
Britain, 4, 10, 17, 27, 35–6, 40–1, 46, 48, 77, 111–12, 118; British Empire, 12; *see also* UK
British Guiana, 19, 23
Brixton, 118
Brixton to Barbados, 136
Brooklyn, 111–12, 115–16
Brooklyn Themes, 111, 113, 115
Brown Jr, Larry 'Blue', 62–3
Brown, Lloyd, 87
Burnham, Forbes, 66
Bye, Erik, 118, 120, 122–4, 126, 127n.20, 138, 149
Bynoe, Margaret, 115, 116, 149

Calling the West Indies, 28
calypso, 34–5
Calypso Rose, 112
Campbell, Ambrose Adekoya, 34–5
Campbell, Owen, 20-2, 28
Cane Hall, 74, 76
Carib, 66, 98, 126
Caribbean, 3–4, 9, 17, 19, 23, 28, 31, 34–5, 39–40, 47, 53, 66, 76, 78, 81–2, 85–8, 92, 100–1, 105, 111–12, 117, 123–5, 130–1, 140, 150
Caribbean Voices, 20, 22, 28, 57, 84, 129
CARIFESTA, 66, 69n.21, 78, 118
Casa de las Américas, 25, 76, 82, 102
Cato, Milton, 72–3
Cato, Vin, 15
Cerra, Steven, 60
Césaire, Aimé, 22
Chalkey, 112
Charles, Jonathan, 19
Chatoyer, Chief Joseph, 126
Civil Service Association, 74
Clarke, Kenny, 62
Clarke, Petula, 58
Clayton, Peter, 40, 79, 116, 149
Coasters, 31
Coleherne (pub), 38
Coleman, Ornette, 46
Collymore, Frank, 20, 23, 27–8
Cologne, 58, 60, 61, 62
Colombie, SS, 27
colonial, 10, 15, 40; administration, 10, 13, 19, 24n.17; anti-, 18; education, 40, 84; elite, 76; lands, 22; life, 83; loyalty, 12; outpost, 4
Commonwealth Institute, 63
Compton, John, 57
creole, 21, 106; creolisations, 102
Cyril McIntosh's Brass Band, 9
Cyrus, Sir Cecil, 16–18, 23, 30, 77, 84, 129, 149
Cyrus Emporium, 16

Daisley, Darrow, 15
Dankworth, Johnny, 32
Davis, Miles, 31, 36–7, 55
Department of Culture, St Vincent, 72, 96
diaspora, 4, 111, 115, 123
Dickinson, Mary, 119, 121
Dixieland, 55
Dominique, Joe, 150
Dorsey, Tommy, 13
Duke, 112
Duke of Wellington (pub), 120
Dyer, Geoff, 117
Dynely's Rehearsal Rooms, 29

Edelhagen, Kurt, 58, 60–2
education, 13, 15, 18, 28, 84, 88–9, 99
Education Forum of the People, 68, 72
Egypt, 60, 85
Eliot, T. S., 86
Ellington, Duke, 9, 35
Empire Day, 12–13, 15
Empire Windrush, 27

England, 1, 4, 20, 27, 30, 38, 40, 57, 83, 114, 117, 125, 148–9
English, 8, 9, 14, 16, 18, 31, 36, 39, 40, 45, 76, 83, 85, 86, 123; literature, 9, 16, 18, 29
Europe, 1, 4, 16, 24, 29–30, 40, 49, 58, 63, 68, 77, 96, 111, 141

federation (regional), 4, 12, 19, 66
Fishnet Bar and Restaurant, 75
Flamingo, 29, 33, 120
Florian, Sara, 105, 106
France, 62
Frangipani Hotel, 74
Fraser, Adrian, 75, 117, 148
Fraser, Cadman, 13
Fraser, Stilton 'Stilly', 76–7

Ganda, Ali (Lord), 34
Garrick, Michael, 36–7, 40, 46, 52–5, 57–8, 66, 95, 117–19, 124–5, 149
Garrod, Sarah, 150
Gaynair, Wilton 'Bogey', 60
Gelly, Dave, 30
Georgetown, 2, 11, 15, 23, 75, 89
Germany, 3, 49, 55, 58–60, 62–4, 74, 82
Ghana, 34
Gibbs, Tony, 32
Gillespie, Dizzie, 31, 35–7
Girls' High School, 74–5
Goode, Coleridge, 31, 38–43, 46–7, 49, 55, 63–4, 117–20, 124, 138, 149

Goodman, Benny, 13
Gowers, Patrick, 30
Greggs, 74
Grenada, 11, 23
Grier, Selwyn MacGregor, 11
Grime, Kitty, 45, 113
Guyana (*see* British Guiana), 19–20, 22, 23, 29, 66

Halperin, Daniel, 44
Hampstead, 57
Harkavy, Anthony, 30
Harlem All Stars (*see also* All Stars), 31 39
Harriott, Joe, 31–3, 36, 38–9, 41–9, 51n.43, 54–5, 59–60, 67, 118, 124–5; *see also* Joe Harriott Quintet
Hastings Girls Choir, 40
Hathaway, Martin, 118
Heidegger, Martin, 117
Henderson, Russ, 38
highlife, 34–5
Highlifers, 35–6, 45
Hobsbawm, Eric, 47
Holt, Rev E. J., 15
House of Nehesi Pubishers, 116, 149–50
Hughes, Ted, 55
Hull, University of, 29

identity, 5, 19, 29, 82–3, 98
immigrants, 27–8, 47
independence, 4, 34, 72
India, 34, 64

Intermediate High School, 75
Italian/Abyssinian war, 18
Ixion, 23, 82, 86, 92n.8

Jackman, Oliver, 57
Jamaica, 23, 28, 119; Jamaican, 20, 38, 61, 78, 87, 98; Jamaicans, 45
James, Canute, 46
James, C. L. R., 57
jazz, 1, 3, 5, 16, 29–32, 36, 38–42, 45–8, 51n.40–1, 52–8, 60, 62, 64, 76–7, 81, 83, 87, 92, 95–6, 102, 104, 106–7, 112–13, 117, 120, 122–5, 147–9
Jazz News, 36, 44
Jazzgalerie Club, 63
Joe Harriott Quintet, 29, 31–3, 36, 38, 43, 45–6, 48–9, 58, 116, 118, 125; see also Harriott, Joe
John, Kenneth, 21, 68, 74
Johnson, Linton Kwesi, 78–9, 95, 113, 118–21, 150
Joshua, Ebenezer, 19, 72–3
Joshua, Ivy, 73

Keane, Alan, 29, 63–4
Keane, Charles E, 7–8, 11–12, 15, 24n.7
Keane, Christiane, *née* Ricard, 29, 57, 60, 63–5, 68, 69n.16, 71, 112, 128, 149–50
Keane, Darnell Mendelssola, 7
Keane, Donny, 7, 11
Keane, Dorcas Maude (*née* Edwards), aka 'Jessie', 7–8, 15

Keane, Edna Elaine, 7, 111
Keane, Ellsworth, 122
Keane, Hadassah, 7
Keane, Magdalin Roxann, 7
Keane, McIntyne Wilberforce, 7
Keane, Noel Julian, 63, 64, 65, 69n.19
Keane, Theodore Vanragin, 7
Keane, Van, 112
Keane family, 8–9, 11, 13, 63
Keating, Johnny, 35, 58
Kenton, Stan, 60
King, Cheryl, 148
King, Errol, 148
King, Martin Luther, 58
Kingstown, 1, 7–11, 13–19, 21–2, 69n.9, 75, 116, 125–6, 148–50
Klein, Harry, 48
Kurt Edelhagen Orchestra, 49, 60–1, 68
Kuti, Fela, 34
Kyk-Over-Al, 20, 23, 85

L'Oubli, 21, 23, 82, 86
'Lady' boats, The, 19
Lamming, George, 29, 117
LaPage, John, 28
LaRose, John, 75, 97, 112, 119, 150
Lawrence, Gene, 32, 77
Lawrence, Ted, 13, 15
Le Gendre, Kevin, 125
Lee, Laurie, 55, 57
Legislative Council, St Vincent, 10–12
Lloyd, Ruth, 114

INDEX

London, 3, 17–20, 24, 28–30, 32–5, 37, 39–40, 42, 46, 52–4, 57–9, 63–8, 75, 82, 88, 95, 97–8, 112–13, 115–21, 124–5, 149–50
London University, 18, 30, 53–4
Lucerna Palace, 60

McGranahan, James, 8, 40
McIntosh, Frankie, 112, 117, 148
McIntosh, George, 19
McIntosh, Harold, 15
McIntosh, Tom, 15
McKenzie, Mike, 31, 39, 48
Marks, Natasha, 105
Marquee Club, 31–4, 48, 53, 120
Marryshow, Albert (Teddy), 19
Marson, Una, 20
Martinique, 14, 22
masculinity, 5, 30; black, 31
Mellow Tones, 15
Melodisc, 35
Melody Maker, 38, 46
Melody Makers Steel Band, 9
Methodism, 53; Methodist, 13; Methodists, 8
Methodist Church, 13–14, 125
Methodist School, 14
Miami, 113
Michael Garrick Quintet, 58
middle class, 14
migrant, 47, 68, 96–7, 124; migrants, 4, 19, 29, 47, 98; migration, 4–5, 24, 97–9, 116
Miller, Glen, 13
Milligan, Spike, 55–6

Mitchell, Sir James 'Son', 17, 56–7, 64, 68, 71–6, 88, 148
Mittelholzer, Edgar, 29
MM (blogger), 35–6, 56
Moore, Hilary, 39, 46
Murphy, Rosalie, 83
music – Nigerian, 34; rock, 47; sacred, 53, 57–8 (*see also* jazz)

Naipaul, V. S., 28, 82
nationalism, 3, 5, 83
nationalism, black, 21
nature, 83, 85, 88
New Beacon Books, 75
New Democratic Party (NDP), 74
New York, 3–4, 78–9, 81–2, 87, 110–18, 120, 122–3, 125, 148–9
Nkrumah, Kwame, 34
Norway, 3, 118, 120, 122–3, 149; Norwegian, 98, 122–4
Notting Hill, 39, 63, 65, 119
Nurse, Rupert, 34

Orr, Bobby, 43, 118
Oslo, 120, 122–4
One A Week With Water (OWWW), 82–3, 88–9, 99, 101

Peace Memorial Hall, 116, 126
Pendleton, Harold, 32, 34
People's Political Party (PPP), 72
philosophy, 53, 84–5
Pick, Muriel 'Lou', 68, 74–5
Pinewood Sanatorium, 39
Pixley, Dick, 29

poetry, 3, 5, 9, 21–3, 28–9, 36, 52–7, 66, 76, 81–7, 92, 95, 99, 102, 105–6, 112–13, 119, 123–5, 149–50
Pound, Ezra, 86
poverty, 9–11, 17–18, 31
Prague International Jazz Festival, 60
Prescod, Fred, 148

Quebec, 14

racism, 28, 47–8
Ramanan, Elizabeth Uma, 64, 68, 71
Ramanan, Roland, 26, 37–8, 47, 59, 64–5, 71, 107, 118, 123–5, 148
Raymonde, Ivor, 35
Reeves Memorial Scholarship Fund, 14
religion, 53, 85; religious, 8, 20, 53, 82, 84–5, 87, 92
Ritzy, 118
Roach, Eric, 87
Robertson, Alan, 46, 48, 124, 148–9
Robson, Jeremy, 52, 54–6, 58–9, 67, 124–5, 149
Rohlehr, Gordon, 87
Rojas, Frank, 15
Ronnie Scott's Club, 45
Royal Festival Hall, 54
Royal St Vincent Police, 8

St Lucia, 22–3, 57, 86
St Paul's Cathedral, 58
St Vincent, 1–4, 10–11, 13–19, 21, 23, 24n.12, 27–8, 32, 65–6, 68, 69n.9, 71–6, 78–82, 84, 88–9, 92, 96–7, 101, 111–12, 115–16, 119, 122–3, 125–6, 133, 147–9; Vincentian, 2, 16, 19–21, 24n.14, 28, 45, 68, 76–7, 82, 92, 98, 101–2, 105, 112, 125, 148
St Vincent Labour Party (SVLP), 72–3
St Vincent Philharmonic Orchestra, 15
Salkey, Andrew, 28
Sampson, Joe 'Chet', 35
Samuels, Winston, 15
scholarships, 13–14
Scottish, 45, 64
Seamen, Phil, 35, 42, 45, 51n.43
Sekou, Lasana M., 150
Selvon, Sam, 28, 82
Seymour, Arthur J, 20, 22, 23, 85
Shake, Beat and Dub, 118
Shaw, Hank, 41
Sierra Leone, 34
slavery, 31
Small Axe, 106
Smith, John, 55
Smith, Leo, 15
Smythe, Pat, 33, 42, 46, 51n.43
Soho, 31–2
Soso, Winston, 112
Soufrière, La, 88–9
Stephenson, John, 148
Stitt, Sonny, 35, 37
Sunset Club, 32
Sutherland, Rowland, 125

Swanzy, Henry, 20, 22, 27–8
Switzerland, 62
Syncopators Steel Band, 9

Taylor, Johnny, 55
Taylor, Samuel Coleridge, 40
Telemaque, Harold, 22
Teupen, Jonny, 62
The Southside Six, 30
The Vincentian, 16, 20, 74
The Volcano Suite, 79–80, 82, 88, 90
Themen, Art, 30
Theosophical Society, 53
Thomas (grandson), 136
Thomas, H. Nigel, 148
Tiffany's Lounge, 113, 115
Toronto, 76
Trinidad, 22–3, 27–8, 69n.21, 77; Trinidadian, 34, 112
Trunk, Peter, 62
Tufnell Park, 63

UK, 65, 125; *see also* Britain
unemployment, 11, 27
United States, 31, 42, 63, 79
University College London, 29
University of the West Indies, 21, 68

volcano, 80, 88, 90

Walcott, Derek, 22–3, 40, 85–6, 100
Wall, Anthony, 78, 118
Walter, Robert, 10
We See Britain, 28
Wesley Guild, 22
Wesley Hall School, 13
West Africa, 34–5; West African, 34
West African Rhythm Brothers, 34
West India Regiment, 34
West Indian, 19, 21–3, 28–30, 34, 57, 63, 82–3, 85–6, 98, 106, 125; West Indians, 27–8, 32, 48, 63, 98; West Indies, 24, 85, 150
Westdeutscher Radiofunk, 58, 62
Wheeler, Kenny, 49
White, Sarah, 75, 112
Williams, Blazer, 73, 75
Williams, Daniel (Danny), 19–22, 28
Williams, Frank, 15
Williams, Henry, 15
Williams, Jonelle, 150
Wilmer, Val, 36, 38, 43, 96, 113–15, 149
Wilson, Kenny, 33
Windward Islands, 11
Winkler, Anthony, 82
working class, 11, 28
Working Men's Co-operative Association (WMCA), 11
World War Two, 72
Wright, Denny, 35